A Practical Guide to Living in Japan

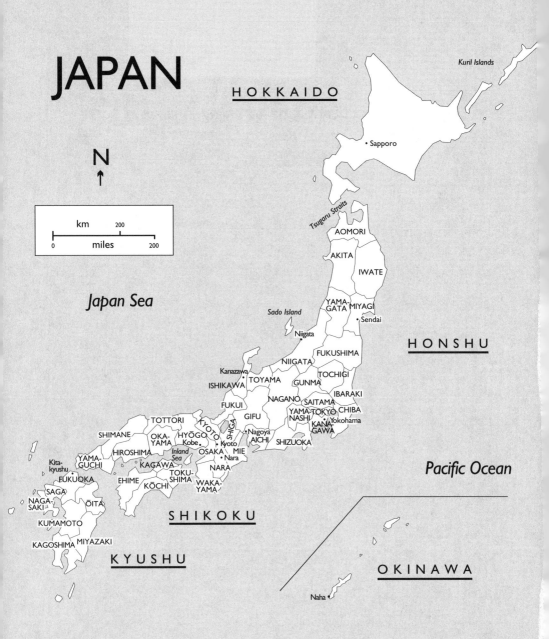

JAPAN

HOKKAIDO

N

| km | 200 |
| miles | 200 |
0

• Sapporo

Kuril Islands

Japan Sea

Tsugaru Straits

AOMORI

AKITA

IWATE

YAMA-GATA

MIYAGI

• Sendai

Sado Island

• Niigata

FUKUSHIMA

HONSHU

NIIGATA

Kanazawa

TOCHIGI

ISHIKAWA

TOYAMA

GUNMA

IBARAKI

FUKUI

NAGANO

SAITAMA

CHIBA

TOTTORI

GIFU

YAMA-NASHI

TOKYO

• Yokohama

KYOTO

SHIGA

• Nagoya

KANA-GAWA

SHIMANE

OKA-YAMA

HYŌGO

Kobe

AICHI

SHIZUOKA

YAMA-GUCHI

HIROSHIMA

Inland Sea

OSAKA

MIE

• Kyoto

• Nara

Pacific Ocean

Kita-kyushu

KAGAWA

NARA

FUKUOKA

EHIME

TOKU-SHIMA

WAKA-YAMA

SAGA

KŌCHI

SHIKOKU

NAGA-SAKI

ŌITA

KUMAMOTO

OKINAWA

KAGOSHIMA

MIYAZAKI

KYUSHU

Naha

A Practical Guide to Living in Japan

Everything You Need To Know To Successfully Settle In

JARRELL D. SIEFF

Stone Bridge Press • Berkeley, California

Published by
Stone Bridge Press, P. O. Box 8208, Berkeley, CA 94707
tel 510-524-8732 • sbp@stonebridge.com • www.stonebridge.com

NOTE TO READERS: Regulations, procedures, addresses, and phone numbers change frequently. Information contained in this book was believed to be correct at the time of publication. Neither the author nor the publisher can be responsible for any loss or damage from the use or misuse of information contained in this book. Please send corrections and updates for future editions to sbp@stonebridge.com or to Guide@TanabataImports.com.

Printed in the United States of America.

10 9 8 7 6 5 4

ISBN 1-880656-50-7

Contents

About This Book

This book has been prepared to help anyone who is planning a stay in Japan or who has just arrived in Japan and is planning to live there for three months or more. Students living on their own, business persons, and people juggling personal interests or hobbies (like studying martial arts) with jobs like English teaching will all find information here to help them attend to important daily-life details like finding a home, buying furniture, setting up a bank account, and so on.

The presentation is organized more or less by the sequence of necessity, with immigration procedures taken up first, followed by home hunting, hooking up utilities and getting your bearings, opening up a bank account, and arranging for health care. These subjects are followed by brief introductions to jobs and schools and public transportation. I've provided a fairly detailed section on buying a car, since many people moving to Japan, especially English teachers on government- or privately sponsored programs, do not live in major cities but in rural areas where public transportation is less convenient and car ownership is advantageous. I've also included a brief rundown on common situations where proper etiquette must be observed. As in all things Japanese, you will learn the most if you are patient, observant, and inquisitive. Do not hesitate to ask your Japanese friends and colleagues for advice and for help, especially when you are just starting out.

At the back of the book is a compilation of important phone numbers and addresses. These are believed to be current and correct, but bear in mind that offices close or move locations from time to time.

One of the best sources of information about living in Japan is the Internet. There are dozens if not hundreds of sites that provide information, tips, addresses, instruction, recipes, reading lists, and just about anything else you may be looking for. I have not devoted a lot of space to listing Internet sites because these change frequently and in any case are fairly easy to find using standard Internet search engines. Some of the most useful sites for the purposes of this book are in Japanese only, but there are usually English-language sites that discuss topics in enough detail to be useful. Internet cafes, if not your very own computer, can thus be an important lifeline to you in Japan, as well as a supplement to what is contained in this book.

Pronouncing Japanese

Japanese words appear in this book both in their romanized forms (that is, written in English letters) and in Japanese script, which includes *kanji* (the pictographic-style characters) and two phonetic syllabaries, *hiragana* and *katakana*. Pronouncing Japanese is not difficult, and each letter in the romanized spelling is sounded much as it is in English. Vowels are pronounced as follows:

a as in "father"
e as in "pet"
i as in "Hawaii"
o as in "open"
u as in "flute"

A vowel with a line (called a macron) over it ($\bar{o}$, $\bar{u}$) is sounded twice as long as a regular vowel.

The letter *r* is flapped to sound between an *r* and an *l*.

A final *n* creates a nasal, as in *hon* (meaning "book").

The letter *g* always represents a hard *g*, as in "get."

The letter *f* is more like a breath blown out between the lips.

A double consonant is held for a brief stop before the rest of the word is pronounced: *kappa* = *kap . . . pa.*

Japanese syllables should be pronounced with even stress (unaccented)

Note that Japanese words and geographical names in common use in English (Kyoto, Osaka, Kobe, Tokyo, etc.) are written as they are in English, that is, without long signs to indicate extended vowels.

Currency and Money

The value of the Japanese yen (¥), although fairly stable over the last few years, fluctuates, sometimes by as much as several percent in a month. Prices in Japan are always changing too. You will have to decide the best strategy for when to convert funds you bring from your country into yen. You can track daily conversion rates on the Internet at sites like www.xe.com.

Acknowledgments

This book is dedicated to all of the teachers of Japanese who have devoted their lives to educating others and helping to build the bridge between the East and West.

I would especially like to thank Aya Kaneko and the Kaneko family, Rachel Braaten, Masamichi Matsushita, Seika Matsushita, and Conor O'Scannlain, without whose help this book would not have been possible.

J.D.S.

Off to the Land of Wa

So you're off to the land of *Wa! Wakoku* (和国) is another name for Japan. *Wa* (和) means harmony and *koku* (国) means country or land. You have probably seen pictures of Japanese temples surrounded by trees in the vibrant colors of autumn or pictures of serene Japanese women dressed in immaculate kimono performing tea ceremony with practiced technique. Or perhaps on television you have seen chaotic Japanese train stations during rush hour or busy Tokyo intersections during weekends. It is hard to know exactly what to expect with so many contradictory images coming from Japan into the Western media. You can decide for yourself whether Japan is a country of harmony or not. But the longer you live in Japan the more you will notice a striving for social harmony that is quite unique to Japan. And the longer you live in Japan, the more you will learn about the character of the Japanese people and how they think and feel. As you do, you can adapt to your new home and develop your own feeling of *wa* with Japan.

You will never forget that you are a foreigner while you are in Japan. This has both its good points and bad points. The Japanese will always excuse you for not knowing their customs, culture, or language and will almost expect you not to know any of their customs, culture, or language. Whether your venture is teaching English, going to school, or working at your company's Tokyo branch office, Japan will teach you new perspectives and habits on an almost daily basis. When you arrive in Japan, you may find it amusing to see Japanese people bow when talking on the phone. After six months or so, you'll find yourself bowing when talking on the phone. You will slowly pick up Japanese ideas and behavior, and before long you'll come to think and act differently from how you did before. When you return to your home country, don't be surprised if you still bow when on the phone, or are bothered by people not taking their shoes off when entering a house. This means you were successful in adapting to a Japanese way of life.

Japan can be a very pleasant country to live in. When asked to describe Japan to those who have never been there, I always respond, "Which Japan? Tokyo or the rest of Japan?" Although they share the same language and foods, Tokyo and the rest of Japan are two extremely different environments. Your experience as a foreigner will depend on where you live. The countryside, or *inaka* (田舎) as Japanese call it, is more or less anywhere outside of Tokyo. The big city of Osaka, of course, is not considered the countryside by people who live there, but whether this is true or not Tokyoites and Osakans have debated for generations.

Living in the countryside has its ups and downs. If you live in the countryside, you will be famous. People will be extraordinarily nice to you, probably invite you over for dinner, and generally want to get to know you better. Chances are you are one of the first foreigners to reside in the area. Your new neighbors will want to learn more about you and your culture. Although rent and daily living expenses are for the most part cheaper in the countryside, you do not see the amazing variety of goods and services found in Tokyo. However, if you adopt a more Japanese-country lifestyle, you will realize that you do not really need expensive imported products. Living in the countryside you will probably learn more of the language. Since there are fewer English-speaking Japanese and even fewer foreigners there, you have an excellent chance to receive for free what other Japanese-language students spend tremendous amounts of money on. Finally, in the countryside you will experience more traditional Japanese culture. Although Tokyo has its festivals and traditions, they are always a little different from local festivals in a small town or village, where you will be the celebrity foreigner receiving all kinds of special attention as the locals teach you the rituals that have been passed down for generations. Living in a small town, in other words, will make your experience in Japan unique.

Tokyo is one of the largest metropolitan areas in the world. It has fewer parks than any of its industrialized counterparts and is crisscrossed by several different webs of train and subway systems. It lacks the serenity of the countryside and at times feels like a real concrete jungle. Tokyo has its perks though, and they are good ones. Absolutely anything is available (for a price) within forty-five minutes travel. You can find most any kind of foreign cuisine, clothing, books, and magazines. Stores are open late, sometimes all night. There is a greater variety of entertainment and it is easier to stay in touch with the Western world since there are so many foreigners residing in the Tokyo area.

Whether you live in the countryside or in Tokyo, one of the main reasons it is so easy for a foreigner to live in Japan is the people. Japanese are anxious to teach foreigners their culture and their language. It is relatively easy to make Japanese friends, even if you do not speak a word of their languge. Take advantage of your time in Japan by studying some cultural tradition, like the tea ceremony or aikido, and you will acquire a greater appreciation and understanding of Japanese culture and values.

I highly encourage anyone who is going to live in Japan to study the Japanese language. It makes everyday living infinitely easier. Japanese know that their language is difficult for foreigners to learn due to its complicated writing system. They will be impressed if you can speak Japanese, almost to the point of being patronizing. This is because until recently not many Westerners could speak Japanese. This has changed with Japan's economic success and the consequent career opportunities for foreigners there. Today, there are thousands of English-speaking foreigners in

Japan, many of whom can speak Japanese very well. It is quite easy to get around Japan without knowing a word of Japanese, but if you do not speak at least a little of the language there will always be missed opportunities as well as problems you cannot solve by yourself.

The Weather

The Japanese archipelago is located around the center of the temperate zone, so while the weather is generally mild, it is characterized by pronounced seasonal changes. Warm winds blow off the Pacific Ocean, making it very hot and humid in the summer, while in the winter winds blow cold off the Asian continent. The weather varies depending on where you live. A long range of mountains runs lengthwise down the main island of Honshu, making regional climates quite distinct.

Summer begins with *tsuyu* (梅雨), the rainy season. In Tokyo, *tsuyu* usually runs from the beginning of June to the latter half of July, but these dates vary from year to year. The rainy season starts in the southern region of Kyushu and gradually works its way up through the country, but usually does not reach the northern island of Hokkaido. At this time, Japan is showered by light rain all day long, and you can get thoroughly soaked just walking to the local train station. Large thunderstorms are rare, but the constant light rain is more than enough to keep you constantly wet. Count on spending a lot of time walking outside. Japan's excellent transportation system is the main mode of transit, but using it requires a walk or bicycle ride to the train station. Most Japanese do not wear raincoats or parkas, but almost everyone has an umbrella.

Tsuyu is followed by the hot summer, which usually lasts until mid- or late September. Summer is very hot and humid, especially on Kyushu. Even when it may be scorching hot, Japanese rarely wear shorts, although this is changing with the younger generation.

Spring and autumn are, perhaps, the most comfortable and poetically beautiful seasons. The temperatures are mild with little if any rain or snow. Autumn comes as a nice relief after the hot summer. It is beautiful when the leaves change color, especially in the mountains, and there are all kinds of seasonal foods. Spring is equally gorgeous. Japanese all across the country celebrate the cherry tree blossoms with the important, centuries-old tradition of *hanami* (literally, "flower viewing"). If you are lucky enough to be in Japan at this time, by all means ask a Japanese friend about the best local places to take in cherry blossoms.

The winter season differs depending on what part of Japan you live in. The winters in Kyushu and other parts of southern Japan are quite mild. In Tokyo, it may snow a couple of times a year but the snow usually melts quickly. Occasionally it snows enough to cause the transportation systems to be shut down, but the trains are usually operational again within a day. Northern Honshu and Hokkaido are occasionally hit by heavy snowfalls that paralyze their cities, even with the heavy snow removal equipment intended for these circumstances.

What Should I Bring?

One of the toughest dilemmas when planning any trip to a foreign country is deciding what to bring. This is even more difficult to decide if you are going to be gone from your home country for an extended length of time. First, find out about the weather in the area you are going to and pack accordingly. (You can check out the weather reports for any part of the world, in English, on the web at weather.com.) What you bring also depends on how long you plan to stay in Japan. Most anything you can get at home can also be bought in Japan—usually at a higher price. If you are going to be in Japan a year or less, only bring what you can fit in your suitcases. If you need books, you can save money if you put them all in a box marked "Printed Matter" and ship it by sea; make sure that the box contains only printed matter or the special rates will not apply (the boxes will probably be searched by Japanese customs). Land-to-land shipments take anywhere from one to two months depending on their point of origin. If you plan on living in Japan for an extended length of time you should find a freight forwarder to ship all of your belongings to Japan.

Many foreigners who go to Japan are there for one year or less. If this is true for you, you should be able to bring everything you need on the plane ride over. Here is a brief list of what you may want to bring with you to Japan:

- **Electrical appliances.** Electrical appliances in the Tokyo area work on 50 Hz 100 V. In the Kansai (Osaka–Kyoto) area and all of western Japan, the current is 60 Hz. If you are bringing electrical appliances make sure they are compatible with Japanese outlets, which have only two prongs. If your appliance has a three-prong plug, you can buy a converter in Japan for about ¥1,000. If your home country is on a system other than 100V, you will need a power converter unless the appliance is explicitly marked as compatible with a 100V system. Most computers and many other electrical appliances have internal power converters, but confirm this before you plug in anything.

- **Clothing and shoes.** Before you leave, do some research on the weather of the area where you will be living and choose your clothing accordingly. If you plan on buying clothing in Japan, be aware that it can be difficult to find larger sizes in clothing and shoes there. Since you will do a lot of walking and be expected to remove your shoes when entering homes, bring comfortable shoes that are not too time-consuming to take off and put on.

Most prescription drugs are permitted in Japan. When bringing medications you can bring up to two month's supply of pre-scription medication and up to one month's supply of non-prescrip-tion medication without filling in any paperwork. The same rule applies for medications you received via mail. Bring a copy of the prescription and a letter from your doctor explaining the following: the nature of the medication, the reason you are taking it, the recommended dosage, the frequency of dosage. The following over-the-counter medications are prohibited since they contain stimu-lant ingredients in excess of Japanese standards: Tylenol Cold, Nyquil, Nyquil Liquicaps, Actifed, Sudafed, Advil Cold and Sinus, Dristan Cold "No Drowsiness," Dristan Sinus, Drixoral Sinus, Vicks Inhaler, Lomotil.

- *A Practical Guide to Living in Japan.* Always useful!

- **Dictionary**. Bring a good, portable dictionary or buy an electronic one when you arrive. Each Japanese electronics company markets its own dictionary and all models are small enough to fit into your pocket. Most come with Jap-anese–English, English–Japanese, and *kanji* (Japanese char-acter) dictionaries. These are quite expensive (up to ¥20,000), but they are well worth it. You can purchase such dictionaries at big electronics stores such as Sakuraya and Bikukamera.

- **Pictures**. Bring pictures of your family, hometown, and country to show to the friends you will make in Japan.

- **Homestay presents**. If you plan on living with a family, bring homestay presents. Japan is a gift-giving culture. The price of the gift does not matter. Something unique to your homeland is best.

- **Prescription medication**. Bring at least a six-month supply of any prescription medications you are taking. This will allow you ample time to have your prescriptions re-filled if you run into problems.

- **Books**. Books are best left home (see the comments above if you simply must bring them). Nearly any book that can be purchased in your home country can be found or ordered in Japan. Kinokuniya is a popular bookstore with foreigners and has several locations, not only in Japan but throughout the world. Books can also be ordered via the Internet at www.kinokuniya.co.jp or on Amazon.com.

Computers

Although Japan is one of the most technically advanced countries in the world, the Japanese still do not use computers as much as their Western counterparts. While this situation is changing, computers are still not as accessible as you might think.

If you need a computer while in Japan, it is best to bring one from home. Japanese and American computers are designed to work with different voltages (American systems use 120V). Most newer computers have internal power converters that allow them to work with 100V, but confirm that this is the case with your computer before bringing it. IBM PC and clone users may have to buy an adapter that adjusts the 100V to 50 or 60Hz voltage (depending on which part of Japan you live in). Before you bring your computer, make sure that spare parts can be purchased via the Internet and that repair work can be done in Japan. There are many computer stores with English-speaking staff that sell and fix foreign computers. To find such a a store in your area, refer to an English telephone directory such as CitySource.

Japanese writing and PCs

There are a number of different ways to get Japanese-language capability on your PC. In the past there have been many problems getting Western computers to operate in both English and Japanese. Many of these problems have been weeded out, but it is always a good idea to get the latest upgrades. These are usually available for free on the Internet.

- **Internet and e-mail.** If you only want to view and write Japanese on the Internet or to type e-mail in Japanese, all you need is Japanese Language Support from Microsoft. This can be obtained for free from Microsoft (www.microsoft.com/ie) under Japanese Language Support & Global IME.

- **Japanese in MS Word**. If you want to use Japanese in Word, you will need to get Word2000 or Office2000 and then download and install the same attachments as above.

- **Complete Japanese Operating System**. If you cannot get the Japanese add-ons to work, or if you want a complete Japanese operating system, buy the Japanese version of Windows. You must also purchase switcher software such as PQ Partition Magic or System Commander that allows the computer to operate under both languages.

Japanese Writing and the Macintosh

If you plan to bring your older Macintosh to Japan, you should obtain Japanese-language utilities before you leave home by downloading the Japanese Language Kit from Apple (asu.info.apple. com). Newer Macintosh computers running System 9 and X come with Japanese support built-in. If you want your Macintosh to operate completely in Japanese, you will first need to erase the English system and then install the Japanese system. You should consider this option only if you are very competent in Japanese, as all of the system commands will be in Japanese.

Hanko

Within your first week or two after arriving in Japan, you should have your *hanko* (判子) made. A *hanko* is a name stamp used by the Japanese in place of a signature on official documents. Legally, the signature of a foreigner is just as official as a stamp in Japan, but the problem is that many Japanese do not know this and require a stamp when doing business. To purchase a *hanko*, bring your name written in *katakana* to a stationery store, or *bunbōguya* (文房具屋). *Katakana* are syllabic characters that can be used to approximate the pronunciation of your name in Japanese; if you do not know the *katakana* syllables for your name, ask a Japanese-friend or colleague to write them out for you. *Hanko* usually start at around ¥2,000 but can get very expensive depending on what they are made of. There is no need to buy an expensive *hanko*. A wood *hanko* works just as well as an ivory one.

The *hanko* will usually take a couple of days to acquire since the store has to carve in the *katakana* characters for your name. After you receive your hanko, take it to your local government office to get it registered. Registration will make the stamp official. Once the *hanko* is registered you will receive a proof of registry called an *inkan-shōmeisho* (印鑑証明書). Keep this piece of paper safe since you may be asked for it in situations such as purchasing a car or getting a phone line. The proof of registry is valid for only three months. This is intended to avert any fraudulent uses of the name stamp.

Immigration Procedures

One of the easiest ways to get deported from Japan is to violate an immigration law. If you are caught without a valid visa, you will probably be sent to an immigration control facility (whose conditions are not too different from those of a Japanese prison), where you'll stay until you can come up with the money for a plane ticket home. In addition, you will probably have problems the next time you try to apply for a visa to Japan. Although the Japanese government tends to be easier on nationals from European or English-speaking countries, violating an immigration law is still an unnecessary mess that can be easily avoided.

While in Japan, you are required to carry either your passport or your alien registration card (see below) at all times. Japanese police officers have the right to ask to see your passport or alien registration card and search you without probable cause. Sometimes just being a foreigner is cause enough. This is especially true if you do not look Japanese. Remember, foreigners stick out in Japan, and you're especially conspicuous if you wear anything the Japanese might stereotype as suspicious: funky clothing, sunglasses, a beard, tattoos, and so on. Although things are starting to change, the Japanese police do not have a lot of experience with foreigners and may assume that just because you are a foreigner you are committing crimes. Try not to be too offended if you have an unpleasant encounter with a Japanese law officer. A large number of crimes in Japan actually are organized and committed by foreigners. Japan is one of the safest countries in the world, and

Japanese police take every measure to maintain this high standard. Japanese regard the lax safety standards of a country like the United States as something to avoid.

If you happen to be searched, speak as much Japanese as you can and show the police everything they ask to see. Japanese police will usually treat you politely and respectfully even while they search you for weapons or drugs. The more polite and cooperative you are, the sooner the whole process will be over.

Visas

Unless you are from a country such as the United States or Canada, which has a tourist visa agreement with Japan, you must obtain a visa before entering Japan. Register at the nearest Japanese embassy or consulate in your country and receive a certificate of eligibility (actually a stamp in your passport indicating the proposed status). You must arrive in Japan within three months of the date of issuance. It is extremely important that you have this stamp when entering Japan; otherwise you will probably be asked many questions upon arrival and sent back home on the next flight. There are different requirements for different nationalities, so make sure you find out all the relevant information for your own case (for example, U.S. citizens do not have to apply for a tourist visa at a Japanese embassy in the U.S. since they are automatically granted a ninety-day visa upon entering Japan; but make sure this rule is still in effect before you leave).

If you are already in Japan under a tourist visa you must leave the country in order to change the status of your visa. Foreign nationals used to go to the Japanese embassy in Seoul, Korea, since that is the embassy closest to Japan. Lately, Japanese immigration has been enforcing the rule that one must obtain the visa from an embassy or consulate general in one's own country. Therefore, unless you are Korean, going to Seoul may not be a good idea. It all depends on how busy the immigration officials are and what mood they are in. American citizens should keep in mind that there is a Japanese consulate in Guam.

There are several different types of residency status in Japan, each granting different privileges. These include:

diplomat	official	artist
college student	religious activities	journalist
professor	researcher	medical services
instructor	engineer	cultural activities
trainee	entertainer	skilled labor
pre-college student	temporary visitor	dependent
intracompany transferee	legal/accounting services	other designated activities
specialist in humanities /international relations	investor/business manager	

Check with the embassy or consulate in your country to find out the prerequisites for each of these visas.

Alien Registration
外国人登録証明書

gaikokujin tōroku shōmeisho

All foreigners residing in Japan must register as foreign aliens within ninety days of entering the country (with the exception of foreign nationals who enter Japan temporarily for transit purposes, tourists, those who fall under the Japan-U.S. Status of Forces Agreement, and diplomats and their families). The process is quite simple but extremely important. The alien registration card is necessary to receive a re-entry permit, a Japanese driver's license, or any national health insurance coverage. Register at the nearest local ward, municipal city office, town office, or village office. The card easily fits into your wallet or purse and must be carried with you at all times. You are required to show it to any immigration officer or police officer upon request. Once you obtain this card, you are no longer required to carry your passport.

If you are registering for the first time, bring your passport along with two 3.5 x 4.5 cm photographs of your face full front from the shoulders up (you cannot be wearing a hat). For children under sixteen years old, no photograph is required. You must fill out the appropriate documents (unless you will be residing in Japan for less than one year), and you will then receive a temporary alien registration card. Within two weeks you must return to the office and pick up the laminated alien registration card.

Do not forget to carry your alien registration card with you at all times. The Japanese police may demand to see this card at any time, and it can be a hassle if you do not have it on you. Children fifteen years old and younger will be issued their foreign registrations immediately. For foreign babies born in Japan, the birth certificate must be submitted to the same office. Any changes made after the issuance such as a change of address, employer, visa status, authorized period of stay, or issuance of a new passport must be reported within fourteen days. Also, if you lose your registration card, you must apply for reissuance within fourteen days.

Your certificate of alien registration is valid for five years. The expiration date is written on the front side of the card. Within thirty days of the expiration date, your local ward will send you a reminder that your registration is about to expire. Before the expiration date, go back to the local ward or government office and register again. The procedure is the same as above.

You are required to return the alien registration card at the point of departure such as customs at the airport (unless you have a re-entry permit or a refugee travel document). If an alien is granted Japanese nationality or dies while in Japan, the card must be returned to the place of issuance within fourteen days.

If you have any questions about any of these applications or procedures, you can call the General Information Center for Foreign Residents at (03) 3213-8523 or the Foreign Residents Advisory Center at (03) 5320-7744.

To find the immigration offices and information centers nearest you, see the section "Important Phone Numbers and Addresses" at the back of this book.

Re-entry Permission
再入国の許可
sainyūkoku no kyoka

Re-entry permits are required for all foreign nationals who wish to leave Japan and come back under the same status. You must get a re-entry permit any time you leave Japan or your current residence status will be canceled upon your return. You can purchase a re-entry permit at some airports, but it would be wiser to get it at the immigration office. The airport may take too much time and you risk missing your flight. A re-entry permit is good for the amount of time remaining on your visa, with a maximum of one year (four years in the case of special permanent residents). If you leave Japan and cannot re-enter for a justifiable reasons, such as illness, you may be granted an extension of one to two years (five years in the case of special permanent resident). If you plan on leaving and returning to the country frequently it might be a good idea to get a multiple re-entry permit since a single permit is ¥3,000 and a multiple permit, which is good for unlimited re-entry within the confines of the expiration date, is ¥6,000.

REQUIRED DOCUMENTS

- application for re-entry (available in English at the immigration office)

- your alien registration card

- your passport (or, if you do not have a passport, you must submit documents explaining the reason)

- in case of application for multiple re-entry permission, materials supporting the necessity of multiple re-entry

All applications must be made in person unless this is impossible due to old age, illness, or other physical impediments, or if the applicant is under the age of sixteen. In these situations, applications can be obtained by proxy by the applicant's mother, father, spouse, or the person who has care of the applicant. For those who are living in Japan permanently, there are designations of permanent resident, spouse or child of Japanese national, spouse or child of permanent resident, and long-term resident. Under these categories, immigration control puts no limitations on your activities. Check your local Japanese embassy or consulate to see if you can qualify for any of these designations.

Resident aliens receive their residence status upon entering the country. A foreign national who has not gone through entry procedures (for example, someone who was born in Japan) must apply for and acquire residence status if he or she is to remain in Japan for more than sixty days.

Special Residency Requests

Whenever you deal with immigration authorities, make sure you do everything properly and on time. The following are some of the situations in which special permission is required from immigration control:

If you do not have a visa but you want to work and live in Japan, consider finding a job at a language school before coming to Japan. The Japanese government grants visas quite easily to foreigners who teach their native language at language schools. Many foreigners find a job through one of these schools, come to Japan under an instructor's permit, and then look for another job while teaching at their school. The money you can make teaching a language in Japan can be enough to support yourself until you find the job you are looking for. Once you find a new job with a company that will sponsor you for your visa, go through the procedures for changing your visa outlined in this chapter.

1. *Permission to engage in any activity other than that permitted by the residency status previously granted (shikakugai katsudō no kyoka, 資格外活動の許可)*

This situation includes part-time jobs for college students, whether it is tutoring English or working at the local sushi restaurant. Teaching English can be a good source for extra income, but is only legal if the instructor has the right visa (an instructor or specialist in humanities/international relations visa or special permission). No foreign national under a tourist visa may legally engage in any kind of work without this special permission. There are many bar hostesses and English tutors who are not aware of this law. Although it may seem easy to get away with, keep in mind that if caught without the proper visa, you are going to have an unpleasant time with the Immigration Bureau, and this could impede any future application for a visa in Japan.

REQUIRED DOCUMENTS

- application for permission to engage in activity other than that permitted under the previously granted residency status (2 copies)

- materials indicating, in concrete terms, the nature of the activity to be engaged in (for example, a copy of your employment contract or a brochure describing the business of your employer)

· materials indicating the nature of the activity presently engaged in (for example, the enrollment certificate of a foreign student)

2. Permission to change residency status (zairyū shikaku no henkō no kyoka, 在留資格の変更の許可)

This is required of anyone who wishes to change the status of a visa, such as a college student who graduates and then wants to become an English teacher.

REQUIRED DOCUMENTS

· application for change of residency status (2 copies)

· a statement of reasons for making the application

· materials indicating in concrete terms the nature of the new activity to be engaged in (for example, a copy of your letter of admission and financial documents proving your ability to bear all expenses necessary during your stay in Japan)

3. Permission to extend period of stay (zairyū shikikikan no kōshin no kyoka, 在留敷期間の更新の許可)

A foreign resident who wishes to stay under the same residency status beyond the period granted needs special permission. This must be done before the original expiration date. An application for an extension of the period of stay will be accepted from about one month prior to that date. Anyone who stays in Japan beyond his or her authorized period of stay without special permission is subject to punishment and deportation.

REQUIRED DOCUMENTS

- application for extension of period of stay (2 copies)

- statement in concrete terms of the activities presently engaged in and reasons why the extension is required

4. Permission for permanent residence (eijū kyoka, 永住許可)

An individual who wishes to change residency status from temporary to permanent must get special permission. This is difficult to acquire. According to Immigration, the applicant's residency in Japan should be of such a duration that the foundation of the person's life has become deeply rooted in Japanese society. Permanent residence is permitted only when a foreign national has established a permanent base of livelihood and it is deemed that his permanent residence will be in accord with the interests of the nation. More concretely, this means that the person has significant assets or the ability to make an independent living (not required for spouses and children of Japanese nationals, special permanent residents or permanent residents, or those who have been recognized as refugees) and that the person is of good conduct (not required for spouses and children of Japanese nationals, special permanent residents, and permanent residents).

REQUIRED DOCUMENTS

- health certificate (including HIV status)

- materials showing that the applicant has sufficient assets or the ability to make an independent living

- materials showing the applicant's behavior has been good (not required for spouse and children of Japanese nationals, special permanent residents or permanent residents)

- documents certifying family relations (family registration and so on)

Immigration problems—late renewals, missing paperwork, incomplete applications—can cut short your stay in Japan and land both you and your sponsor in serious difficulties. Always make sure your forms are complete. Adopt a patient attitude and accept the fact that you may sometimes be at the complete mercy of an immigration clerk. It is in general helpful to have an established Japanese citizen—a business person or teacher, for example—speak to Immigration on your behalf if there is a complicated problem that needs to be sorted out. Many Japanese are reluctant to step into a situation if they do not know you well or if it may create a deep obligation. So if someone does help you out, be aware that rendering assistance is for them not a casual matter and be sufficiently appreciative of their efforts.

5. Permission to acquire residency status (*zairyū shikaku no shutoku no kyoka*, 在留資格の取得の許可)

Residency status is available to those individuals who were born in Japan and those who renounce their nationality and desire to remain in Japan. The application must be made within sixty days. In the case of newborns, the application should be made by the father, the mother, the person who cares for the infant, or anyone who lives with the infant.

REQUIRED DOCUMENTS FOR NEWBORNS

- application for permission to acquire residency status (2 copies)

- documents certifying birth

- questionnaire (available at the Regional Immigration Bureau)

REQUIRED DOCUMENTS FOR OTHER REASONS

- application for permission to acquire residency status (2 copies)

- statement of reasons for the application (a document showing the specific reasons for the necessity of acquiring residency status and indicating the activity to be engaged in after acquisition)

- documents certifying the above reasons

- materials explaining the activities to be engaged in after acquisition of residency status

Foreign nationals who wish to cancel their passports when they acquire Japanese nationality, foreigners who have obtained a new passport and need to transfer the endorsements, and foreigners who have a certificate of authorized employment (established by the amendment of the Immigration Control Act, effective since June 1, 1990) must take all passports, old and new, to the Immigration Bureau. If the old passport is lost or destroyed, only the new one must be submitted.

Finding a Home

Trying to find a place to live can be one of the most frustrating experiences for a foreigner in Japan. There are many reasons for the difficulty. Many Japanese landlords have not previously rented to foreigners, and some fear that foreigners will leave before the contract expires, requiring them to find new tenants. They are thus apprehensive about communicating and negotiating with foreigners and, given the choice, would rather rent to Japanese. It is not illegal to discriminate on the basis of race or nationality in Japan, and many landlords do not hesitate to do so. On top of this, most foreigners do not have experience renting in Japan. The Japanese apartment rental system can be confusing, especially if you do not have a trustworthy Japanese friend who can help explain the procedures and formalities. Foreigners often rent apartments they do not necessarily like because they do not know what else is available. As Japanese become more accustomed to dealing with foreigners in Japan, and as foreigners come to understand the Japanese system better, it should become easier for non-Japanese to rent an apartment. For the present, we must do our best to establish mutual trust and understanding.

Accommodations for Fresh Arrivals

Staying in Japanese hotels can be expensive, especially if you have to stay in one for a few weeks while searching for an apartment.

Luckily, more affordable accommodations are available. Business hotels are scattered throughout Japan at a fraction of the price of most normal hotels. The rooms are not fancy, but there is a daily cleaning service, usually a small TV, and occasionally a refrigerator.

Another option is the *ryokan* (旅館), a traditional Japanese-style inn. These are small Japanese-style houses or sections of a house turned by the owner into a small hotel. *Ryokan* frequently cost a fraction of the price of a hotel and provide more personal service. Almost all of the rooms are Japanese-style with futons to sleep on, plenty of closet space, and a small table. The price of a *ryokan* includes one or two meals a day. If you choose to stay at an inn in the countryside, the owner may even take you out for drinks or dinner. *Ryokan* offer a unique and pleasant experience. Even if you do not stay in one upon your arrival, by all means try one out while you are traveling through Japan. But be aware that some *ryokan* are extremely expensive and designed for wealthy guests seeking a sophisticated traditional environment.

Two more options are pensions and *minshuku* (民宿), small Japanese hotels for travelers. These are similar to *ryokan* but are run more like hotels in that the service is not as personal.

One of the cheapest (and easiest) options is to stay at a *gaijin* (foreigner) house (外人ハウス). These apartment buildings, which resemble college dormitories, are specifically intended for foreigners. The landlords are used to dealing with foreigners and will probably speak English. The *gaijin* house is a good alternative for those on a tight budget or the very newly arrived. It is considerably cheaper than an apartment since you do not have to sign a two-year contract. Rooms are rented by the month, or, in some cases, by the week, or even by the day. There is no "key money" (move-in fee) and no penalty for moving out on short notice. *Gaijin* houses are good for individuals but completely unsuitable for families (most *gaijin* houses won't allow children anyway). If you decide to stay at a *gaijin* house, don't have high expectations; you get what you pay for. You will not have much privacy and you may have several roommates (this may be okay for a young person not yet established in Japan). *Gaijin* houses are often advertised in the classified sections of English-language newspapers and magazines.

A final option for families or individuals who need a temporary residence is the short-term apartment. This is rented out by the week or the month for any length of time. To find listings of phone and fax numbers for these apartments, look under "Apartments" in the CitySource English Telephone Directory published by NTT. If you have not yet arrived in Japan, you can find a copy of this phone book at your local Japanese Consulate General's office, JETRO office, or Kinokuniya bookstore. Many listings are also available on the Internet.

Apartments

Apartments (*apaato*, アパート) are usually rented through real estate agents, whose small offices have apartment listings (*bukken-harigami*, 物件張り紙) taped to the windows or signboards out front. These printed strips of paper contain information such as the distance to the nearest train station, the age of the building, and the initial move-in costs. A housing information journal (*jūtaku-jōhōshi*, 住宅情報誌) can be purchased at most kiosks and bookstores. Another good source of apartment ads is the Monday edition of the English-language newspaper *The Japan Times*.

There are many factors to consider when searching for an apartment. The closer the apartment is to a train station or the center of the city, the more expensive the rent. In Tokyo, it is much more expensive to rent an apartment inside the circle of the Yamanote Line than it is in a suburban area. If you do not mind long commutes and crowded trains, you can save a small fortune by living in the suburbs. You may also want to note whether the apartment is near a school, hospital, or railroad tracks, where noise may be a problem.

Apartments are usually rented under two-year contracts, but shorter terms are possible. If it is likely that you will not be able to stay for an entire two-year term, make sure that this is all right with the landlord before signing a contract.

Most foreigners rent an apartment or what is called a *manshon* (マンション). An apartment can be one room without a bathroom/shower, or it may be a couple of rooms with a bathroom/shower. Japanese apartments are usually intended for a single person and are less expensive than a *manshon*. A *manshon* is more suitable for a couple or a small family. Do not be misled by the word, which comes from the English "mansion." A *manshon* is simply a larger and more expensive apartment. It may have more rooms or be in a newer building (see the illustrations on pages 36–37).

It can be quite expensive to move in. Due to the rental system in Japan, the renter may have to pay as much as several months' rent in advance. However, negotiating the key money, rent, and deposit is possible, especially in times of recession. The following is a list of typical charges and payments associated with moving into a new apartment:

- **Monthly rent** (*yachin*, 家賃). Rent is paid monthly, usually through a bank. To learn how to pay rent, refer to the section about transfers in the chapter "Bank Accounts and Postal Accounts." Many contracts allow the landlord to cancel the contract if rent is late more than once.

- **Down payment** (*tetsukekin*, 手付け金). Usually two weeks' to one month's rent is paid flat out to the landlord. This fee guarantees the execution of the formal contract and will not be refunded if the contract is canceled at the renter's request. This deposit is part of the payment made to the landlord upon signing the contract and will be applied to the first month's rent or the key money (*reikin*) after the contract has been signed.

A Western-style Japanese apartment.

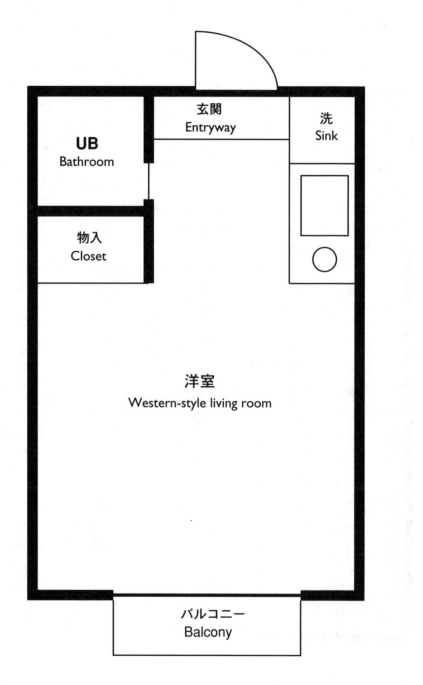

UB
Bathroom

玄関
Entryway

洗
Sink

物入
Closet

洋室
Western-style living room

バルコニー
Balcony

A Japanese-style apartment or manshon.

LDK
Living
Dining Room
Kitchen

バルコニー
Balcony

洗濯
Washing machine

便所
Toilet

玄関
Entryway

洋室
Western-style room

廊下
Hallway

Closet

物入   物入

外廊下
Outside corridor

ユニットバス
Unit bathroom
(shower, tub)

脱衣洗面
Changing room and sink

和室
Japanese-style room

Closet

押入   押入

- **Key money** (*reikin*, 礼金). One or two months' remuneration fee paid to the landlord. This is a charge to the tenant that will not be returned. Not all landlords require key money, especially if the apartment is on the expensive side.

- **Damage deposit** (*shikikin*, 敷金). Two to six months' rent paid as a refundable deposit. If no damage is done to the apartment, the full amount will be returned when you move out.

- **Realtor's fee** (*chūkai assenryō*, 仲介斡旋料). One month's rent paid to the real estate agent as a service fee. By law, real estate agents are not allowed to charge more than one month's rent.

Fees vary from apartment to apartment and agent to agent. A monthly maintenance fee (*kenrikin*, 権利金) may be charged, and if a parking place is included, a parking fee may be charged (if no space is needed, the parking fee can, of course, be waived). All of this information is contained in the *bukken-harigami*. Although moving into an apartment can be expensive, most, if not all, of the deposit money will be returned when you move out.

As with most things in Japan, there are both Japanese and Western styles. There may not be any difference in their architectural layouts, but there are important aesthetic and design differences. For instance, a Japanese-style apartment will have tatami mat floors. Tatami mats are also the unit of area measurement, whether the apartment is Japanese or Western style. Each tatami mat unit is called a *jō* (畳) and is approximately 1 x 2 m. The Japanese apartment's cabinets (*oshi-ire*, 押し入れ) are also Japanese style for bedding storage; in a Japanese-style apartment the proper and most common bed is the futon, which is folded up and put away in the closet each morning to maximize space.

A Western-style apartment will have either a wood or carpeted floor. If you want a Western-style bed, you can purchase one at most department stores. A futon can, of course, be used in a Western-style apartment and is much cheaper, and actually more comfortable than, most Western-style beds available in Japan.

Reading the Bukken-Harigami

Thanks to the *bukken-harigami,* it is easy to shop around for different apartments without actually talking to a landlord or an agent. The window of every real estate agent's office is plastered with these little information-packed fliers.

Each *bukken-harigami* has different information. Some of them have only the dimensions of the apartment and required costs for moving in, while others have everything from the age of the building to the name of the utility company serving that area. Many of the words contained in the *bukken-harigami* may be difficult to find

A typical bukken-harigami, *with English translations.*

新宿駅歩１０分

10 minutes walking from Shinjuku Station

礼金　１ヵ月 —— 1 month *reikin*　air cond. included ＊エアコン付

敷金　２ヵ月 —— 2 months *shikikin*　intercom —— ＊インターホン

駐車所　12,000 円 —— parking spot fee

＊静な住宅地

雑費　1,000 円 —— miscellaneous fees　quiet neighborhood

契約期間　２年　（更新可）

room number

	203	202	201
	86,000	84,000	86,000

contract period　2 years　(renewable)

rent

no dogs, cats or pianos

1.犬猫、ピアノ不可
2.更新料は新賃料の１ヵ月分

contract renewal fee is one month's rent

in a dictionary since, to conserve space on the flier, the real estate agent may use one *kanji* character to represent a whole word or phrase. Here is a list of useful terms with common *kanji* abbreviations in parentheses:

ENGLISH	ROMANIZATION	KANJI (ABBREV.)
air conditioning	*eakon*	エアコン
address	*jūsho*	住所
apartment	*apaato*	アパート
apartment flier	*bukken-harigami*	物件張り紙
balcony	*barukonii*	バルコニー
children not allowed	*kodomo-fuka*	子供不可
communal services fee	*kyōkihi*	共益費 （共）
contract	*keiyaku*	契約
contract period	*keiyaku kikan*	契約期間
corner room	*kado heya*	角部屋
damage deposit	*shikikin*	敷金 （敷）
dining room/ kitchen	*DK*	DK
down payment	*tetsukekin*	手付け金
entryway	*genkan*	玄関
foreigner house	*gaijin hausu*	外人ハウス
hallway	*rōka*	廊下
housing	*jūtaku*	住宅
housing info journal	*jūtaku jōhōshi*	住宅情報誌
intercom	*intaahon*	インターホン
Japanese-style room	*washitsu*	和室 （和）
key money	*reikin*	礼金 （礼）

landlord	*shujin*	主人
living/dining room/kitchen	*LDK*	LDK
maintenance fee	*kenrikin*	権利金 （権）
maintenance fee	*kanrihi*	管理費 （管）
mansion	*manshon*	マンション
miscellaneous fees	*zappi*	雑費 （雑）
one-room apartment	*wanrūmu*	ワンルーム
outside corridor	*gairōka*	外廊下
real estate agency	*fudōsanya*	不動産屋
realtor's fee	*chūkai assenryō*	仲介斡旋料
renewable (contract)	*kōshinka*	更新可
renewal fee	*kōshinryō*	更新料
rent	*yachin*	家賃 （賃）
room number	(__) *gōshitsu*	(__)号室
shower	*shawaa*	シャワー
toilet	*benjo*	便所
unit bath	*UB*	UB
washing machine	*sentakki*	洗濯機 （洗濯）
washing/dressing room	*senmen*	洗面
Western-style room	*yōshitsu*	洋室 （洋）

Other key phrases and kanji

(#) minutes from station to bus stop by bus	バス [#] 分
(#) minutes from bus stop to apartment	歩 [#] 分
(#) minutes walking from the station	駅歩 [#] 分
[ ] included	[ ] 付

[ ] not included   [ ] 無

[ ] not allowed   [ ] 不可

[#] months' rent required for *reikin, shikikin,* etc.   [#] カ月

To avoid misunderstandings, know everything that is written on the *bukken-harigami* of any apartment you look at. If you do not feel confident communicating in Japanese, ask a Japanese friend to come to the real estate agent with you. Many real estate agents do not speak English. It will make life easier for everyone involved if you or someone with you speaks Japanese.

Finding Furniture

Most apartments in Japan are unfurnished, and, unlike unfurnished apartments in the U.S., usually lack even a stove, heater, and refrigerator. Furnished apartments are occasionally available, but the rent for them is higher and the quality of furniture is often poor. Furnished apartments are usually intended for the short-term renter who does not want to acquire furnishings for just a few months' use.

Almost any furniture you need can be purchased at a department store, but the prices may be higher than at your neighborhood store. Buying used furniture can save you a lot of money. Here are some ideas for places to find affordable furniture.

- **Department stores**. Almost everything you would ever need for your apartment can be found at a department store. Delivery service from department stores for larger items is usually free, but you will have to wait at your apartment on the appointed day of delivery. Time-designated deliveries are uncommon.

- **Neighborhood stores**. Neighborhood stores are generally cheaper than department stores. There is less selec-

Once you move in, you should give a gift to the landlord as a token of appreciation for taking you in. It does not have to be expensive. It could be tea or sweets (okashi), or better yet, something from your own country. You should also pay your new neighbors a visit with a small gift. You will probably not be invited in since Japanese people are not very comfortable with letting people into their apartments, especially someone they are meeting for the first time. Do not be surprised if they greet you at the door and take the present without any overtures.

tion, but what you find is usually adequate for furnishing your first apartment.

- **Classifieds**. At the back of most magazines for foreigners living in Japan, like *Kansai Time Out, Tokyo Classified,* or *Tokyo Weekender*, you can find listings for used furniture.

- **Local universities**. Universities have a high turnover rate, and students are always trying to get rid of something. Check university and dormitory bulletin boards.

- **www.licus-sk.com/used-fur.html**. You can buy cheap used furniture over the Internet. This web page is in Japanese, but it is fairly easy to understand, since you just have to match the picture with the price.

- **Street shopping**. You can often find discarded treasures put out for recycling, such as lamps, small electronic goods, and even tables and storage units.

- **Flea markets**. Flea markets are another resource that can save you a lot of money. Since a law was passed in Japan allowing fees to be collected on the disposal of household appliances and other large items, flea markets have become more abundant and popular throughout Japan. Flea markets are held at different locations on certain days depending on the month. Check local foreigners' magazines to see listings of flea markets in your area. Here is a list of a few Tokyo flea markets:

Katsushika-Nishi Recycle Center	(03) 5670-2992
Nakano Recycle Center	(03) 3387-2411
Omori Recycle Center	(03) 3774-3811

What to Buy for an Apartment

Here are the essentials for furnishing your new place:

Beds or futon
The first thing you need to purchase is a bed, blanket, sheets, and pillows. Futons are the most comfortable and least expensive kind of bedding to buy in Japan. They fold up neatly into the closet, which makes the apartment much more spacious during the day. Western-style beds are also available but tend to be quite uncomfortable, especially fold-up sofa beds. Japanese beds may be shorter than what you are used to; always check mattress length before you purchase.

Air conditioner
You will want to have an air conditioning/heating unit. This is a roughly 1.3 x 0.5 m remote-controlled box. If your apartment does not have one, you may have to buy one (about ¥90,000–¥120,000) and have it installed. You can also buy a little space heater—electric, gas, or kerosene—but this can be expensive and dangerous to run.

Washing machine
Japanese washing machines are plastic, flimsy, little high-tech devices usually placed on the veranda of an apartment. Some apartments may already have a washing machine, most likely because

the prior tenants didn't bother to take it with them when they moved out. If there is already one in your apartment and you are happy with it, great. Just make sure you run at least one cycle with nothing but bleach before you use it. If you are not lucky enough to get an apartment with a machine, you will probably find a laundromat in your neighborhood. As a temporary measure, this is much cheaper than buying a new washing machine and is nice if you want to dry your clothes in a dryer (most Japanese hang-dry their clothes outdoors). If your new home has no washing machine and there are no laundromats nearby, you will have to buy a machine. If you plan to be in Japan for fewer than three years, one of the cheaper machines will suffice.

Refrigerator

Base the size of the refrigerator you buy on the size of your apartment. Most people living in apartments and smaller manshon have half-sized refrigerators to save space. Your apartment may come with a refrigerator (again, probably because the prior tenant left it there).

Dishwashers

Dishwashers are not generally used in Japan. Space in most Japanese kitchens is limited, and washing the dishes by hand takes only takes a couple of minutes.

Kotatsu

A *kotatsu* (こたつ) is a low Japanese table with a heating unit underneath. During the winter, you drape the frame of the unit with a large, square blanket (*kotatsu kake buton*, こたつ掛布団) and then place a table top over the frame. Several cushions are placed around on the tatami (or carpet) so that you can sit with your legs under the *kotatsu* to keep warm during the cold winter months. During the summer, the blanket is removed and the *kotatsu* can be used as a regular table.

Couch or zabuton

You will need a couch or the little Japanese cushions (*zabuton*, 座布団) for you and your guests to sit on.

Vacuum cleaner

The longer your stay, the better the vacuum cleaner you will want. Make sure it is strong and can fold up neatly to fit into your closet.

Telephone

With all of Japan's high-tech appliances, there is a great variety of telephones and multi-purpose telephone/answering/fax/copy machines (*takinō denwa*, 多機能電話) that can be purchased at electronic stores. Purchasing a phone line to use these devices, however, is a complicated and expensive process; see the chapter "Utilities" to learn how to purchase a phone line.

Kitchenware and dishes

Kitchenware can be bought at neighborhood stores and department stores at fairly low prices.

Utilities

Utility usage can be expensive in Japan, but you will quickly learn to adjust your habits to keep costs under control. Japanese homes and apartments do not use central heating. If you keep your entire home heated in the winter and air conditioned in the summer, you are going to have some pretty big electricity bills. With the deregulation of Japanese international phone service, phone bills are cheaper for foreigners than they used to be. However, you can still spend a lot of money if you do not watch the clock when talking on the phone. Learning to do without some of the luxuries you had back home and altering your daily habits a little can save a considerable amount of money.

After moving into your apartment you will need to set up your utility services. Most apartments will already have the gas, water, and electricity set up when you move in, but speak with the landlord to make sure. Except under special circumstances, phone service is never included in an apartment rental agreement. You will need to make a separate contract with the phone company to get phone service.

Home Phones

Getting phone service in Japan is expensive because phone lines must be purchased. To buy a new phone line, you must go to the nearest NTT (Nippon Telegraph and Telephone, the national phone company) office with a form of identification such as your passport or your alien registration card. Including the nonrefundable charge to purchase the phone line, the subscription charge, the installation fee, and a 5 percent consumption tax, the initial hookup will cost around ¥80,000. You can get a portion of this money back when you leave Japan by selling your line to someone else. Also, you can save a considerable amount of money if you buy a used phone line. To find listings, look in the classifieds of local magazines for foreigners. Make sure that all bills on the phone line have been paid by the seller or they will be carried over to your account.

To have your phone line installed you must arrange an appointment with NTT. It is important that someone is home the day of the hookup to let the phone company workers in. You can purchase the actual phone unit from any discount electronics store, where prices are negotiable, or you can rent one from NTT for a small price.

NTT also offers a number of optional services for a small monthly charge:

- touch-tone line service including voice-mail service

- reservation service for seats on JR trains for those living in the Tokyo area

- airline reservation service and a bank and securities brokerage answering service

- call-waiting and call-forwarding services

Telephone Tips

Here are some useful numbers provided by the phone service via touch-tone phone:

NTT Repair service	113
Collect calls	106
Telegrams within the country	115
Time signal	117
Weather forecast	177
Directory assistance	114

Emergency phone numbers are as follows:

| Police | 110 |
| Fire and ambulance | 119 |

If you move while in Japan, call 116 as soon as you can to make an appointment for reinstallation. There is an installation charge that varies depending on the work required in addition to the 5 percent consumption tax. These charges will be included on the next monthly bill. Your phone number may remain the same, or it may change depending on where you move. After you get a new phone number, you can have your new number announced by a recorded message when a call is made to your old number.

You can have NTT hold your telephone rights for up to five years without being billed for the monthly exchange line charge. However, you will not be able to keep your previous telephone number when it is reconnected unless you pay the monthly exchange line charge. When you do not need your telephone line anymore you can give your telephone rights away or sell them.

To transfer the title of the telephone, you must go to the NTT office that controls your line with the following documents:

- application form with the signatures of both yourself and the new subscriber (available at any NTT office)

- your certificate of signature or your name stamp (if you cannot get the certificate of signature, you must bring some other document of identification such as your alien registration card, passport, or driver's license)

- the new subscriber's photo identification

When you apply for telephone service, you will automatically be set up with long distance service providers. You can use any of the long distance carriers from your home at any time by simply dialing the appropriate number (listed below) before the phone number of the party you want to call. Each company has different

Japanese long distance carriers charge extremely high prices for international calls. For international calls, I would recommend getting a callback service that costs a fraction of the price the Japanese carriers charge. To be eligible for callback service you need to have a foreign credit card to which your calls can be charged. How it works is simple: you dial the phone number of the callback service, and when you hear a tone you dial your account number and then hang up. Within ten seconds your phone will ring and you will hear a dial tone; you then dial the phone number as if you were in the country you are calling. This way foreign rates will apply instead of Japanese rates. The Japan Times is full of advertisements for these companies.

rates for different countries, so you'll have to investigate to find which one best suits you.

- KDDI

Direct dial	001
Operator-assisted calls	0051
Information	0057

- Cable & Wireless IDC

Direct dial	0061
Information	0066-11

- Japan Telecom

Direct dial	0041
Information	0088-86

Portable Phones

There are two portable phone systems in Japan, cellular phones (*keitai denwa*, 携帯電話) and the Pocket Phone System (PHS). The cellular phone is more expensive but has more capabilities. You can use it in almost any urban area, inside cars and trains, and you can make international phone calls. NTT DoCoMo provides an i-mode cellular phone service. An i-mode phone is a cellular phone with a small screen that is connected to the Internet. Subscribers are charged according to the volume of information transmitted. With an i-mode phone subscribers can use the phone as a phone, for e-mail, and for web surfing. They can also do banking, ticketing, credit card inquiries, and mobile trading, and use travel and entertainment services such as reservations, restaurant guides, network games, and even fortune telling. Package plans and prices differ depending on which local company you choose.

The PHS system may be better for those who want a more affordable phone service. This is how the PHS system works: when a phone call is made, it is transmitted from the base center to receiving dishes placed throughout the city and then to your phone. For this reason you can only use it in places with a dish nearby. In larger cities, dishes are placed throughout the streets, at stations, department stores, restaurants, and so on. There is much more interference with PHS, and you cannot make international phone calls, but, at a fraction of the price of a cellular phone, it is not a bad option.

To qualify for these services you must present your passport and foreign registration card, and you must have been in Japan for at least 120 days prior to purchasing the service.

Needless to say, the telecommunications scene in Japan, like elsewhere, is changing fast, and new services are being offered all the time. Talking to people or looking at recent newspapers and magazines will be the best way of figuring out which service or technology to choose.

Pocket Bells

Pocket bells (pagers) are also available throughout the country. Inquiries and applications can be made at your local NTT office or at any DoCoMo office. There are different pocket bells available at prices ranging between ¥2,000 and ¥3,000 per month with a ¥5,000 deposit and a ¥3,000 handling fee. The deposit will be returned upon cancellation.

Public Telephones

There are several kinds of public telephones (*kōshū denwa*, 公衆電話). Most are green and take phone cards that can be bought for

¥500, ¥1,000, ¥5,000, and ¥10,000 from vending machines, station kiosks, and department stores. It is a good idea to keep one in your wallet or purse since they are convenient when you do not have proper change. To use a phone card, just pick up the receiver and push the card in the appropriate slot. A number will light up showing the remaining credits. When the credit reaches zero, you will hear a couple of beeps warning you that you are about to be disconnected. Phones with gold plates accept phone cards and are capable of making international calls.

Not all phones take phone cards. If the phone is green but has no slot for a card, use ¥100 and ¥10 coins. The phone will not give you change for ¥100, even if you only make a ¥10 call. Carry a handful of ¥10 coins so you do not waste change.

Pink phones are located inside restaurants and stores and are solely for local calls (you cannot even reach the 114 directory assistance number from these phones). These phones only take ¥10 coins.

If you have a power failure, the most likely cause is that the amps being used are higher than specified in your contract with the electric company or you have a short circuit that activated the ampere breaker. Try turning off some of the appliances and pushing the breaker switch up to reconnect.

Electricity

If the electricity is not yet turned on when you move into a new apartment, close the circuit breaker and connect the ampere breaker. If the power still does not turn on, contact the power company whose name is written on the postcard connected to the breaker. After the power comes on, you must fill out the postcard and drop it in the mail. If you move, give the electric company your name, address, moving day, new address, and account number.

Gas

To have the gas in your apartment activated, contact the local area substation before you move and tell them the date you want your service started. There are gas guideline books available in six languages, including English, Chinese, and Korean. Every apartment seems to have its own way of turning the gas on and off, so be sure to have your landlord instruct you. Every year there are fatalities from accidental gas explosions. If you smell gas in your apartment, turn off the supply valve and open all of the windows. Do not light any fires and do not touch electric appliances until you have found the source of the problem and there is no longer any gas in the room.

Water Service

In many apartments, water service is set up by the landlord or custodian. If it is not, you need to contact the Waterworks Bureau substation in your area upon moving in. In case of a leaky faucet contact the Waterworks Bureau substation, and someone will be sent to fix it. If a water pipe bursts, turn off the water supply valve in the meter box. If there is no valve, bind the pipe with a towel. In either case, immediately contact your Waterworks Bureau substation.

Paying Utility Bills

Utility bills can paid in a variety of ways. You can have bills automatically paid from your bank account. To set this up, take to

your bank recent bills from the companies you need to pay, along with your savings account passbook, account seal (if you have one), and your hanko (if you have one). You can also pay bills within a few blocks of your home at post offices and convenience stores. Look on the window or sign at your local convenience store (see the above photo) for company symbols to see which bills you can pay there.

Garbage and Trash Collection

In Japan you must separate your trash into burnable (*moeru gomi*,

燃えるゴミ) and non-burnable trash (*moenai gomi*, 燃えないゴミ). You may also need to separate your trash into regular trash (*futsū gomi*, 普通ゴミ) and trash such as plastics, rubber, metals, glass, batteries, and so on (*bunbetsu gomi*, 分別ゴミ). Find out where your collection area is from your landlord or neighbors. There should be a sign like the one shown in the photo at left stating what the collection days are for each type of trash. Note which days are regular trash days and which days are for separated trash. The days of the week are represented by the following characters:

Sunday	日	Thursday	木
Monday	月	Friday	金
Tuesday	火	Saturday	土
Wednesday	水		

Never put out trash except on the night before collection, or stray cats and crows will make a mess of it. Place garbage in a container with a lid or a securely tied bag. Glass products, light bulbs, and ceramics must be wrapped in strong paper with the Japanese word for danger—*kiken* (危険)—written on it.

Acceptable trash bags displaying the Environment Cleaning Project Bureau's logo can be purchased from supermarkets or convenience stores. For larger items such as appliances, chairs, mattresses, and so on, you must purchase tickets to stick on the

Buy coupons in the amounts of ¥200 (A) and ¥300 (B) and affix them to your trash. The chart at bottom left shows how many coupons you need for typical household items. A futon is one A coupon, a TV is an A plus a B coupon (total ¥500), and so on.

有料粗大ごみ処理券A	1枚200円	
有料粗大ごみ処理券B	1枚300円	
処理手数料	主 な 例	貼付する処理券(シール)
200円	ふとん、椅子(応接椅子除く)等	A1枚
500円	TV(20インチ未満)、カーペット、自転車等	A1枚・B1枚
800円	冷蔵庫(高さ80cm未満)、電子レンジ等	A1枚・B2枚
1,400円	TV(20インチ以上)、タンス(高さ90cm以上)等	A1枚・B4枚
1,900円	冷蔵庫(高さ80cm以上)、両袖机	A2枚・B5枚
特大・70リットル相当	1セット 5枚 (1枚378円)	1,890円
大 ・45リットル相当	1セット10枚 (1枚243円)	2,430円
中 ・20リットル相当	1セット10枚 (1枚108円)	1,080円
小 ・10リットル相当	1セット10枚 (1枚 54円)	540円

item. There are two types of tickets, A and B; A costs ¥200 and B costs ¥300. The tickets can be purchased at convenience stores, and you may have to purchase more than one ticket for an item. A futon is the cheapest item to dispose of at one A Ticket, while a refrigerator is the most expensive at two A tickets and five B tickets (totalling ¥1,900). Then contact the Environment Cleaning Project Bureau (*sōdai gomi shori gyōsha*, 粗大ごみ処理業者) in your ward office and they will arrange a day for your items to be picked up. Ask your neighbors or landlord about recycling projects and flea markets in your area where you can donate usable items that you no longer need.

Settling In

After moving into your new home, the first thing you should do is get familiar with your new neighborhood. It is extremely easy to get lost on Japanese streets. Most of them look about the same, and only the main streets and highways in Japan have names. Addresses are in the form of numbers, with each block having its own set of numbers. It is a very logical system, but it unfortunately makes it difficult to explain your particular address or give directions to people, especially taxi drivers. Keep your address in your wallet or your purse written in the Roman alphabet (*rōmaji*) and in Japanese characters. If a taxi driver has your entire address written in Japanese, there should be no confusion.

Find out where the nearest police box, hospital, and earthquake refuge area are. Learn the way to the nearest stations and the characters and pronunciation of each station, bus stop, and train line you will use. Locate the nearest post office and supermarket. Convenience stores are handy for paying utility bills, and almost every neighborhood in Japan has one.

Japanese Stores

It can be fun to browse through Japan's many different kinds of stores, and they can also teach you a lot about Japanese culture. In department stores, you can see high school girls and college coeds dressed in the trends of the season. If you go to neighbor-

Japanese use bicycles to get around their neighborhoods and to go between their homes and the train stations. You may find a bicycle to be a good investment. It does not have to be an expensive one, as long as it helps you get home from the train station or the grocery store. If you purchase a bike, make sure you get a registry form from the bicycle shop and turn it in completed to your local police station. If you are buying the bike from another individual, its registry form can be obtained from the police station. If you ride at night, there must be a light attached to the front of the bike (especially important since older residential neighborhoods may not have street lights).

hood stores you will be greeted by a friendly, welcoming *Irrashaimase!* (or *Maido!* if you happen to live in the Osaka area). If you come across some strange contraption, ask the store owner what it is for; you will learn more about the Japanese lifestyle.

It is easy to lose track of how much money you are actually spending when you deal in a foreign currency. Try to relate costs to your home currency, but also keep in mind that some things are simply more expensive in Japan. Try to be aware of how much you're spending, but then again, if you always think in dollars the shopping experience can be quite painful.

Restaurants

Japanese take their cuisine very seriously. This can be seen all over in Japan, from the popular television show *Iron Chef* (where famous chefs battle it out) to a popular comic-book (*manga*) series featuring a chef and his cuisine. This love for fine food is reflected in the wide variety of restaurants available in Japan.

On the low end of the price scale are the *ramen* restaurants. A bowl of warm, tasty *ramen* noodles usually costs anywhere from ¥500 to ¥1,000. Large fastfood chains are also scattered throughout Japan, especially near the train stations, so you're set

if you ever get a craving for McDonalds' french fries (in Japan called "Mac fry potato"). Many restaurants display plastic replicas of their offerings in their windows, so you can see what they serve before you enter. This also makes it easier to order if you do not speak Japanese. Higher-priced restaurants usually do not have plastic displays, but menus (with prices) are often displayed by the door.

Make sure you check the prices before entering a restaurant because some are unbelievably expensive, and prices may be (confusingly) written in *kanji* rather than Arabic numerals. Japanese restaurants usually offer a variety of set meals that include a balanced variety of items at a lower price. If you do not like the set menus you can order à la carte. Although Japan has excellent foreign restaurants such as Chinese, Italian, Korean, Indian, French, and American, do not ignore the local cuisine. There are all different kinds of Japanese dishes at all different price ranges, so experiment a little and try something you have never seen before.

The service you get at Japanese restaurants is usually prompt and gracious, even at the fastfood places. Additionally, there is no tipping at Japanese restaurants! There is, however, a 5 percent sales tax; the more expensive restaurants and upscale bars may also charge a table fee.

Department Stores

Department stores are truly a unique experience for visitors coming to Japan for the first time. They have everything from grocery stores to kimono shops to galleries that exhibit world-famous art. Sometimes there will be hosts at the doors and uni-

formed elevator women pushing the buttons and announcing each floor as you arrive. The first level or two of a large department store (often underground) is usually a grocery store. Most items are ordered over the counter, so have a Japanese friend go with you the first couple of times to show you the ropes. It helps if you speak a little Japanese, but most Japanese understand if you point, hold up the appropriate number of fingers, and give them a big smile. The top levels are usually reserved for restaurants, art galleries, and playgrounds. Department stores often deliver large items for free, but you have to wait at your home on the delivery day until they show up.

Supermarkets

Supermarkets are becoming more popular and more abundant in Japan. The prices are often lower than at department grocery stores, and they may be conveniently located near your home.

Convenience Stores

There are several convenience store chains scattered throughout Japan. You can pay your monthly utility bills at most convenience stores, and more of them are getting ATMs each year. Trash collection tickets for large items can also be purchased at convenience stores.

Neighborhood Stores

Japan's streets are lined with small retail shops, especially near the train stations, selling everything from furniture to pottery to paper. These are good places to buy household commodities and utensils. Prices here are lower than at department stores, and the shops may offer free delivery for heavier items.

Discount Electronic Shops

Discount shops such as Sakuraya and Bikukamera sell all kinds of

electronic goods at discounted prices. Many of these discount stores have a membership system where you can earn points to get discounts. Tokyo's Akihabara district and Osaka's Nipponbashi district are full of discounters as well as many other electronics stores. If your Japanese is decent and you have cash in hand, you might be able to negotiate bigger discounts.

Keeping in Touch with Home

As a foreigner in Japan it can be easy to lose track of what is going on in the rest of the world. Japanese newscasters use a lot of difficult vocabulary and speak fast, even for those who have years of Japanese under their belts. You can get newspapers, magazines, and television channels in English to keep you updated on what is happening outside Japan and even to give you a better idea of what is happening inside Japan.

Japan has several English-language daily newspapers that you can use to keep up on world news; these include *The International Herald Tribune/Asahi Shimbun*, *The Daily Yomiuri*, *The Japan Times*, and *The Mainichi Daily News*.

On the Internet you can order the magazines that you normally subscribe to at home through a company called InterMax. Choose from a list of hundreds of different magazines from several different countries (www2.channel.or.jp/intermax). If you do not have access to the Internet, Western magazines, journals, and newspapers are also available at larger bookstores like Kinokuniya or from distributors like:

Intercontinental
Marketing Corporation   (03) 3661-7458

Overseas Courier
Service   (0120) 45-3222

There are also a number of English magazines intended for the foreigner living in Japan such as *Hiragana Times*, *The Nihongo Journal*, *Tokyo Weekender*, and *Japan Select Magazine*. Local magazines published for foreigners, such as *Tokyo Journal* and *Tokyo Classified*, are a good way to learn about local events and to keep in touch with other foreigners.

Television

Sometimes it is nice to watch a little Western TV to remind you that home is still out there. Japan has a few public channels that sometimes broadcast in English (accessible if you have a bilingual TV or VCR). Generally speaking, the number of these programs is quite small. To order cable TV in Japan, go to your nearest electronics store such as Sakuraya or Bikukamera and the staff will help you sign up. SkyPerfect is the cable station for Japan nationally. You can rent a receiver for a nominal price or purchase it from SkyPerfect and then order the specific channels you want. Many channels are free, but most English-language channels (such as Discovery, CNN, or BBC) require a fee. You have your choice of movie channels, sports channels, and children's channels—all for a monthly fee.

Hooking Up to the Internet and E-mail

If all you need is an e-mail account, perhaps the easiest thing to do is set up an account with a company such as Hotmail or Yahoo before going to Japan. These services are free and are accessible from any computer hooked up to the Internet. If you want to hook up to the Internet from your home in Japan, there are a number of service providers like ODN, KDDI, So-net, and AT&T Worldnet. Make sure you close your account in your home country before coming to Japan or you will be charged roaming charges on your old account. Using the Internet in Japan is more expensive than elsewhere, since phone companies charge about ¥10 per two minutes for local calls, although with continuing deregulation, prices are slowly coming down.

The easiest way to get Internet access is to go to the computer section of an electronics store. There will be a display with discs for several different service providers. These should be free (but make sure so that you are not arrested for shoplifting!). Newer Macintosh computers are already Japanese-language capable. Windows-based computers can run Japanese software by installing third-party products over English-language Windows or by installing a Japanese-language version of Windows. If you have problems or inquiries, contact MSN Japan at (03) 5454-8000 and speak with their bilingual operators.

Making Friends

You will find that it is very easy to make friends in Japan. Japanese are genuinely interested in foreign cultures and will be eager to speak with you, particularly in the countryside. Whether it be a tipsy "salaryman" practicing his incoherent English on you or a group of junior high school girls asking you for your autograph, the Japanese sometimes treat foreigners like local celebrities. There are times, however, when you miss talking to someone from your own country or to another foreigner who can relate to problems you may be having in Japan. Don't worry. There are foreigners living in every corner of Japan now. To find clubs and events in your area, go to the foreign-resident section of the public relations department of your ward or city office. Magazines for foreign residents also list several associations in each of their issues. Each prefecture also has an International Exchange Center (*kokusai kōryū sentaa,* 国際交流センター) where you can meet other foreigners living in your area as well as Japanese interested in cross-cultural exchange.

Safety

Japan has one of the lowest crime rates and some of the safest streets in the world. This is one of the first things you will notice on arriving in Japan. Most of the police officers' time is spent giving directions or making sure that bicycles are properly registered. There is a tendency, however, for foreigners to take their personal safety for granted. The crime rate has been going up in Japan, especially gun-related crimes. Also, some cultural differences may make Japan look safer than it is. For example, according to the statistics published in February 1999 by the National Police Agency, in all of Japan there were only 1,652 rapes in 1998. This number would be extremely low for any country. But the truth is that most rapes in Japan go unreported to the police. Additionally, what may be considered a crime in your country may not always be considered a crime in Japan (and vice-versa). In Japan special consideration may be given if alcohol is a factor in a crime, or an arrest may never be made if the offending party makes the appropriate apology.

Japan is such a safe country that it is easy to let your guard down, but you should always take the same precautions you would in your own country. After all, there are dangerous people and dangerous situations in Japan just like everywhere else. Here are a few safety tips:

- Japan is a country that consumes a lot of alcohol. There are situations when you may be expected to drink more than you want. The Japanese generally do not understand alcoholism or nondrinkers in the same sense that we do in the West. Never drink more than you want no matter who is encouraging it. Most likely they are just trying to be hospitable, but it is your body.

- Pay attention at crosswalks. It may look safe to cross the street, but cars pop up out of nowhere from Japan's narrow streets and crowded buildings. Remember that Japanese traffic drives on the left.

- Heed railroad crossing signals. There is a lot of train traffic in Japan, and Japanese crossing signals give you plenty of warning before the trains come. If you hear the bell and the arms are coming down, keep your distance from the tracks.

- Japanese people usually will not go out of their way to help you if you are in trouble. This is a characteristic of their normal behavior, and not because you are a foreigner. Generally speaking, Japanese do not want to get involved or have anything to do with something bad if it is not their business. If you have a problem, the best thing to do is go straight to the police.

- Women should not walk alone at night in deserted neighborhoods, especially near parks. Some neighborhoods may look safe during the day, but the night does bring out some strange and often dangerous people.

- Check the price of any restaurant or (especially) bar before entering, so you will not be tagged with an artificially inflated bill.

- Treat Japan like your own country—that means take all the precautions you would at home. Use your instincts, keep your doors locked, keep your wallet and purse secure; if a situation just doesn't feel right, leave. By using common sense and staying aware of your surroundings, you can avoid most problems.

Tips on Safety on Trains

Trains are the main mode of transportation throughout Japan. You may have seen pictures with stationmasters literally pushing people in so the train doors can shut. This is not a joke. Every year people are hurt, some fatally, while using the trains in Japan. Here are some tips to follow and some problems to be aware of when using the Japanese train system:

- Know your station. Learn what lines to take to get home. Have the name of your station written in *rōmaji, hiragana,* and *kanji* on a piece of paper that you can store in your purse or wallet in case you are lost. If you do get lost, ask a stationmaster for directions.

- Let people get off the train before you get on. If you do not wait, you will not only annoy the people trying to get

There was an English teacher residing in Tokyo who got sick of being fondled on the morning rush hour trains. Her solution, which she claims worked quite well, was to keep a sharp needle at ready in her pocket in case any wandering hands came her way.

off, but you will be trampled by a stampede comparable to the migration of the wildebeest.

· If your trip is for one or two stations, stand near the door. If you are going farther move to the center of the car—it will be less crowded and more comfortable.

· Give priority to elderly citizens, handicapped people, and pregnant women, especially if you are in one of the designated "silver seats."

· Be careful with shoulder-strap purses and backpacks. During rush hour, a purse with a strap can easily get caught in the door. A backpack should be set on the floor or on the luggage rack to give everyone more standing room.

· Do not eat or drink on the commuter trains. Eating is allowed on long-distance trains and in the stations.

· Keep behind the yellow safety line. Some trains fly by fast, especially express trains that do not stop at your station.

· Do not run to make your train. This not to avoid getting stuck in the doors, but rather to save someone from being knocked over in the process, an all-too-frequent event. If you hear the warning bell and everyone around you is running to get to the train, don't worry. There will be another train in a few minutes.

· *Chikan* (痴漢) is the Japanese word for gropers who annoy female train passengers. The rush hour trains are very crowded with everyone scrunched up against each other.

Some men take this opportunity to grope women or girls who are pressed up against them. *Chikan* are one of the main complaints of women who ride the trains. Japanese men are less likely to bother foreign women, but really no woman should let her guard down. Partly due to these complaints, rail services now offer women-only cars.

Earthquakes

Japan has more earthquakes than any other country in the world. If you are there two weeks or more, you will likely experience one. Most earthquakes cause no damage and are over in ten seconds. Large earthquakes, however, can leave sections of cities in rubble (such as the earthquake that struck Kobe City in 1995).

Prepare an emergency kit with the following provisions in a secure place just in case:

backpack	flashlight	raincoat
portable radio	canned food	first aid kit
spare batteries	can opener	bottled water
candles	preserved foods	towel
matches and lighter	cooking pots	soap
knife	blanket	toothbrush and toothpaste

In the event of a big earthquake, observe the following precautions and safety tips:

· Always find out the location of the designated earthquake refuge for your neighborhood and your work place. A list of these shelters can be obtained from your local government office (*yakusho*, 役所).

- Large earthquakes usually last about a minute, so if you are indoors and feel a tremor, the first thing you should do is protect yourself from falling objects by getting under something such as a table.

- Turn off all gas.

- Try to extinguish fires quickly in their early stages.

- Open a door or window to secure an escape route.

- Do not dash outside during an earthquake. There may be falling debris such as glass, signs, and billboards.

- Do not go near narrow roads, walls, or cliffs, which may collapse or give way.

- Be aware of the possibility of landslides or tidal waves.

- Listen to the local English broadcasting channels on the radio or TV to obtain more information or instructions.

If the earthquake is devastating and you have to leave the city on foot, pack as little as possible. Take your emergency kit (you may not need the cooking pots) and wear good walking shoes.

Bank Accounts
and Postal Accounts

For a foreigner, getting a bank account in Japan is a satisfying feeling. When you finally get your own ATM card with your name written on it in *katakana*, you feel you are finally living in Japan—different from all the foreign tourists coming through the country. Opening a bank account is not very difficult to do even if you do not speak a word of Japanese. Usually there is someone in the bank who speaks some English. If your Japanese is good enough, or the teller's English is good enough, then great. But if you are having trouble communicating at a particular bank when trying to set up your account, it may be a sign of greater difficulties to come if and when you have problems. In this case it may be wise to choose a different bank (staffed by people you can communicate with). If there are no banks near you with English-speaking staff and you do not speak Japanese, have a trustworthy Japanese friend go in with you to set up your account.

The larger the bank, the greater the chance it will have experience dealing with foreigners and international transactions. If you live in a country village where there are no banks, open an account in the nearest convenient city. Most banks are open from 9:00 A.M. to 3:00 P.M. and are closed on Saturdays, Sundays, and national holidays.

After opening a bank account, you will be mailed a cash card and personal identification number, or PIN (*anshō bangō*, 暗証番号). The card can be used at ATMs (automatic teller machines) and CD (cash dispenser) machines. CD machines can only be used to withdraw cash, whereas ATMs can be used for withdrawals, transfers, and deposits. You will also get a little bankbook that, when fed into the ATM, will be updated with all of your transactions and your balance. Avoid using ATMs at banks other than your own since they will charge a service fee.

Bank Accounts

Most foreigners in Japan open either a general account or a time deposit account. Checking accounts are usually used only by large companies, almost never for personal accounts.

General Deposits

General deposit (*futsū yokin*, 普通預金) is the most common kind of bank account in Japan. With a general deposit account, you can make deposits and withdrawals at any time free of charge. The interest rate is low, and you can use the account to pay your phone bills, utility bills, rent, and so on.

Time Deposits

With a time deposit account (*teiki yokin*, 定期預金), the interest rate will be slightly higher than with a general deposit account, but you can make cash withdrawals only at certain set intervals such as six months or one year. Before opening a time deposit account, make sure you clearly understand all its restrictions.

Using Cash Machines

Japan runs on cash; checks are used mostly by businesses. Credit cards are becoming more popular every year but are not as common as in many Western countries. Most Japanese carry a rather hefty amount of cash that they use throughout the day to pay for their shopping, groceries, and daily needs. Large transactions such as rent payments are done through bank windows or at ATMs. ATMs and CDs are located all over Japan in banks, post offices, department stores, and convenience stores. ATM operation hours vary from bank to bank. There are no fees for deposits or withdrawals from a branch of your own bank during banking hours; otherwise there is a small charge.

Many cash dispensers and ATMs have a button you can push for instructions in English, but not all machines have this option. If you cannot read *kanji*, keep a piece of paper in your bankbook or wallet with the translation of all the necessary words you need for machine transactions. To make transactions with the bank machines, follow the step-by-step instructions below. If you do not read Japanese, and you live in an area where there are no cash machines with an English option, you may want to memorize the characters needed for your usual transactions. Most banks in metropolitan areas, however, should have at least one machine displaying instructions in English. You can use that until you get a feel for using the machines, and then switch over to a machine that is more convenient to your home or office.

Withdrawals (ohikidashi, お引出し)
1. Push the Withdraw button (*ohikidashi*, お引出し or *harai-modoshi*, 払戻し).
2. Insert your card in the appropriate slot.
3. Enter your four-digit PIN.
4. Enter the amount you want to withdraw. Example: To withdraw ¥35,000, push 3万5千円. 万 means 10,000, 千 means 1,000, 円 means ¥; thus 3 x ¥10,000 + 5 x ¥1000.
5. If you make a mistake, push the Correction button (*teisei*, 訂正). If there are no mistakes, push the Confirmation button (*kakunin*, 確認).

The typical transactions available at a Japanese ATM.

6. If at any time you want to cancel the transaction, push the Cancel button (*torikeshi*, 取消).

Deposits (*yokin*, 預金)

1. Push Deposit (*goyokin*, ご預金 or *gonyūkin*, ご入金).
2. Insert your card in the appropriate slot.
3. When the bank note input door opens, line up the edges of your bank notes and place them in the port.
4. The ATM machine will count the money, and the correct amount should then appear on the screen. If the amount on the screen is correct push Confirm (*kakunin*, 確認); if not, push Cancel (*torikeshi*, 取消).
5. If at any time you want to cancel the transaction just push the Cancel button (*torikeshi*, 取消). Note: Some machines use ◯ for yes and X for no.

Balance inquiries (*zandaka-shōkai*, 残高照会)

1. Push the Balance Inquiry key (*zandaka-shōkai*, 残高照会).
2. Insert your card in the appropriate slot.
3. Enter your PIN. If you make a mistake, push the Correction button (*teisei*, 訂正).
4. After confirming the balance, press the End Transaction button (*torihiki-shūryō*, 取引き終了).

Passbook updating (tsūchō-kinyū, 通帳記入)

1. Press the Update Passbook button (*tsūchō-kinyū*, 通帳記入).
2. Open the passbook to the page of the most recent entry and insert it in the appropriate slot.
3. The passbook will be automatically updated.

Cash transfers (genkin-furikomi, 現金振込)

Cash transfer are typically used to pay bills and fees. Make sure you thoroughly understand how to go through the process of a cash transfer using an ATM machine before attempting it with your account. Have a bank employee walk you through the process step by step and take notes so that next time you can do it on your own. If you do not read Japanese and the machine you are using does not have an English option, make the funds-transfer transaction in person using the appropriate forms and a teller. Below are the commands on a typical machine.

1. Push the Cash Transfer button on the menu (*genkin-furi-komi*, 現金振込).
2. Insert your card in the appropriate slot.
3. Choose whether the transfer will be within the bank or to another bank.
4. Enter the *katakana* syllable of the other bank's name (e.g., *Sa* or サ for Sakura Bank, or *Mi* or ミ for Mitsubishi Bank). The screen will then show (in *kanji*) all the different names for banks starting with that *kana* character. Choose the appropriate bank.
5. Repeat step four to pick the name of the appropriate branch.
6. Enter the account type and account number of the payee.
7. Enter the name of the person who is supposed to receive the transfer.
8. Input the amount you are sending.

9. Input your name and phone number.
10. Confirm everything or cancel.

Using Bank Windows

When you walk into a bank, you will find a counter with a variety of colored forms. The most common forms you will need are those for withdrawals, deposits, and transfers. The highlighted portion is the only part you need to fill out. On pages 75, 77, and 78 are sample forms with translations of the blanks you must fill out. If you have trouble, don't hesitate to ask a bank employee. Whenever making deposits and withdrawals at a bank window, make sure you have your bankbook and *hanko* (name stamp) or you will not be able to make the transaction (these are not necessary, however, if you are just paying bills).

Bank form used for opening a new account.

Opening an account

When opening a new account, have your name stamp and alien registration card; a passport alone will not suffice. Although it is not mandatory, it may be helpful to bring some kind of identification with your work or school address and phone number. A typical new account form is shown on page 75.

Withdrawals and deposits

You can make withdrawals (*ohikidashi*, お引き出し) and deposits (*yokin*, 預金) through the bank window. Pick up the proper forms near the teller's window. Fill in the areas boxed with thick lines. Stamp the appropriate box with your name stamp and give the teller your bankbook. Example forms are on page 77.

Transfers (ofurikomi, お振込み)

To make a remittance through a bank teller, fill out the proper form as shown on page 78. You will need a different form when the recipient's bank is different from yours. Different forms are used for different kinds of transfers, so make sure you use the correct form.

Cash transfers (genkin furikomi, 現金振込み)

A cash transfer is a payment in currency to a third party whose bank may or may not be the same as yours. Hand the teller the completed cash transfer form along with the amount you need to pay plus the bank's service fee.

Direct transfers (kōza furikomi, 口座振込み)

A direct transfer is a payment where the amount owed is debited from your account rather than paid in cash. Fill out the form for direct transfers, stamp the form in the proper area with your name stamp, and hand it to the teller along with your bankbook.

お引き出し（払戻請求書）　普通預金、貯蓄預金、納税準備預金

おなまえ　Name　　お届け印　Name Stamp　様

金額　Amount of Withdrawal

店番号　科目コード　口座番号

ご希望の金種　太枠の中のみご記入ください。

1万円	0,000	¥10,000
5千円	,000	¥5,000
千円	,000	¥1,000
5百円	00	¥500 — Currency Desired
百円	00	¥100
50円	0	¥50
10円	0	¥10
5円		¥5
1円		¥1
計		Total Amount of Withdrawal

別段預金の預入番号

事前決定　決定　事態　決定・検証

内容

現振区分　記帳　決定・検証

現金　振替　混合　日付

出納印　振替相手　当座・普通・貯蓄/定期・通知・別段/本店・損益　口座番号

起票　決定　起票者

番号札　照合者　索引者

納税準備預金払出理由　年　期分　所得申告税・法人税・固定資産税　事業税・物品税・自動車税　市民税・住民税（　税）

Bank form used for withdrawing funds.

お預け入れ　普通預金、当座、貯蓄預金、りぼん、ベスト・ユニット、いずみ、納税準備預金

おなまえ　Name　様

金額　Amount of Deposit

店番号　科目コード　口座番号

金種メモ　太枠の中のみご記入ください。

1万円	0,000	¥10,000
5千円	,000	¥5,000
千円	,000	¥1,000
5百円	00	¥500 — Currency Deposited
百円	00	¥100
50円	0	¥50
10円	0	¥10
5円		¥5
1円		¥1
計		Total Amount of Deposit

ＡＤＳ番号

事前決定　決定　事態　決定・検証

内容

現振区分　記帳　決定・検証

現金　振替　混合　日付

出納印　振替相手　当座・普通・貯蓄/定期・通知・別段/本店・損益

起票　決定　起票者

番号札（カード兼金）　索引者

通調　当手（配当金・利札）枚　他交（配当金・利札）枚　近手（特近）・託手（　）枚　摘要　□振込金受取書発行　□入金帳記入済（帯使用）

Bank form used for depositing funds.

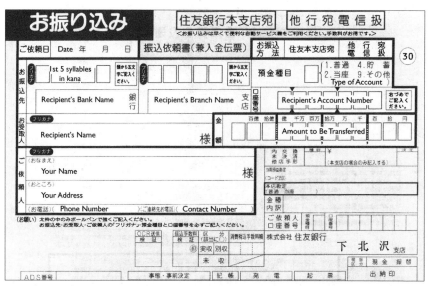

Bank form used for transferring funds.

Sending money overseas through banks

A telegraphic transfer (*denshin sōshin*, 電信送金) is perhaps the safest and the fastest way to send money overseas. You can send a telegraphic transfer in Japanese yen (for an extra charge of ¥1,500), or you can first exchange it in Japan and then send it, subject to local exchange rates, the day of the exchange via check (*yokin kogitte,* 預金小切手). If you exchange the currency it will take four to five days for the regional bank, which deals with foreign currencies, to prepare the check. If you know the payee's bank name and account number you can send it directly to his or her account, but there will be a transfer fee of about ¥3,000 plus other charges. Sending a bank check is more expensive than sending money through the post office, but it is the fastest method.

Postal Accounts

You can also open accounts at the post office. This is a good option if you live in the countryside where banks and ATMs are not readily available. The postal interest rate is slightly higher, and the hours of operation vary. General savings and fixed savings are the most common post office accounts. Even if you open an account through a post office, you still might want to open a bank account for the convenience of the cash machines.

General savings (tsūjō chokin, 通常貯金)

This is, more or less, the postal equivalent of a general deposit account at a commercial bank. The interest rate is slightly higher than at a commercial bank, and although there is a national online service, it is less convenient than the ATM system of a bank.

Fixed savings (teikaku chokin, 定額貯金)

A fixed savings account has a six-month compound interest rate that pays more than the time deposit at a commercial bank.

Sending Money Overseas

You can send money overseas (*kokusai sōkin* or *gaikō yūbin kawase*, 国際送金 or 外国郵便為替) at over 6,600 post offices throughout Japan. All post offices designated as delivery post offices offer this service. In addition, twenty-six Postal Savings Centers (Giro Centers) handle giro transfers between accounts. The currency used depends on the destination. At the post office the amount is converted to Japanese yen and all payments are made in yen. Under Japanese Foreign Exchange Control Laws, you are required to indicate the purpose of the money order (for example, you could simply write "Payment for books" or "Living expenses for someone").

Post offices do not handle payments for services and imports that require permission of the Ministry of Finance or the Ministry of International Trade and Industry, nor do they handle payments for items subject to import control by other laws. The exchange rate is updated daily and is usually more generous than that of a private bank.

Go to the post office and fill out the proper form (*kokusai sōkin seikyūsho*, 国際送金請求書) with the payee's address; do not forget to bring a picture ID. Although this method is much cheaper than a bank transfer, it is slower, and for some foreign countries such as New Zealand it cannot be used. The check can be made out to anyone (except yourself) up to a maximum of ¥500,000. For some countries, there is a service that will let you send money directly from your postal account to a foreign postal account overseas. If you have a giro account there is only a small fee for direct transfers no matter how much is transferred. Since the United States does not use giro accounts, transfers to the U.S. will be slightly higher but still much cheaper than the alternative methods.

There are two kinds of remittances that can be done through the post office: ordinary remittances (remittances by mail) and telegraphic remittances (remittances by telex or telegram).

- **Ordinary remittances**. A money order issued at the post office is sent by the post office through the Tokyo Postal Savings Center via airmail to the designated country. The payee can cash the money order at the post office counter. In the case of money orders sent to the United States, you are permitted to send the money order to yourself. Handling charges vary according to the amount of money sent. Ordinary remittances usually take ten to fourteen days, although it may take a bit longer to certain countries such as Canada, China, or the Philippines. For your protection, any remittance by mail should be sent registered (*kakitome*, 書留).

- **Telegraphic remittances**. Details of the payment are transmitted by telex or telegram to the destination country. The paying authority issues a money order or advice of payment and sends it to the payee. This type of remittance is convenient in urgent cases since it reduces the mailing period to two to four days. The transmission method (telex or telegram) used differs from country to country, and the service is not available in some countries. The handling fee for a telegram is greater than that of a telex, but both are comparable to the cost of an ordinary remittance.

For both ordinary and telegraphic remittances, the payee receives the cash in exchange for the International Postal Money Order certificate at the post office counter. On receipt, no paying charges are levied. In most countries, the money order is valid for three months beginning the month following that of issue. The payee cannot cash the money order after the expiration date.

Giro accounts

Remittances can also be made in Japanese yen, in addition to the home currency, for Austria, Belgium, Denmark, Finland, Germany, the Netherlands, Norway, Spain, Sweden, and the United Kingdom. In the case of yen transfers, conversion into the destination currency will be made in accordance with exchange rates for that currency. When an application form is submitted to a post office or to the Postal Savings Center (Giro Center) managing your account, the remittance amount is debited from your giro account. Conversion from a foreign currency to yen is made on the day the application is accepted at the post office or Giro Center.

Mail Services

The Japanese postal system offers a variety of services in addition to mail. You can pay bills, set up savings accounts (as explained in the previous chapter), and send money overseas as well as New Year's cards to your friends. Post offices are identified by the Japanese postal sign, a red T with a line over it inside a circle.

Japanese postal workers are efficient and courteous. Even if there is a line and people have to take numbers, you will rarely have to wait more than five minutes (except perhaps on the first and last days of the month, when bills and paychecks are paid and cashed). Neighborhood post offices are usually best. Larger post offices and those close to train stations are much more confusing and may take longer to navigate since they have much more traffic.

Orange-red mailboxes with the postal symbol or mailboxes marked "POST" are located all over Japan. The collection schedule is on the side of the box. There are usually two drop slots. One slot is marked for local area mail (for example "Tokyo Area") and the other is marked "Other Areas" or

"International Mail." Outgoing mail should be sent from the post office or a public mailbox. Mail is not collected from home or apartment mailboxes every day, and many home mailboxes become so littered with advertisements from local delivery restaurants that the postal carrier will not take time to look for outgoing mail. The Japanese postal system is quite prompt, with the exception of a few hectic holiday seasons. The operation hours of the post office depend on the area. Generally offices open at 9:00 A.M. and close between 5:00 and 7:00 P.M. On Saturdays they are open until 5:00 P.M., and on Sundays until 12:30 P.M. Postal or giro transfers usually cannot be made on weekends or after 4 P.M. on weekdays.

Addressing Japanese Mail

There is a customary way of addressing envelopes in Japanese just as there is in English. If you write an address in English, use the same format as that used in the United States (starting with the most specific part of the address and ending with the most broad):

1. Name
2. District name and block numbers
3. City town or village name, prefecture name, postal code
4. Country name (not necessary for domestic mail)

Example: Tarō Nakagawa
1-3-2 Shinmachi
Setagaya-ku, Tokyo 154-0014
Japan [if sending from overseas]

If the address is written in Japanese characters, the format is reversed. Reading vertically from right to left the address starts with the most broad geographic designation, the prefecture, and ends with the most specific on the left, the name. You can also

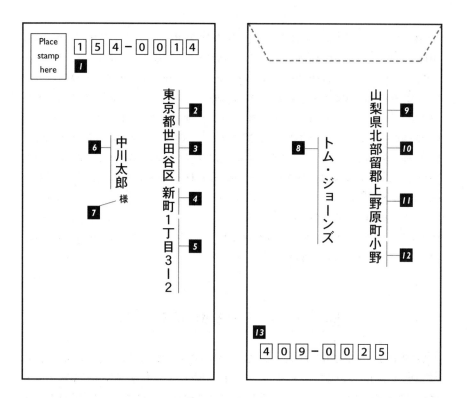

Elements of an address for domestic use within Japan.

1. 154-0014: destination postal code (*yūbinbangō*, 郵便番号)

2. Tokyo-to: destination prefecture (*to, dō, fu,* or *ken*, 都, 道, 府, 県, depending on the type of prefecture)

3. Setagaya-ku: destination county (*gun*, 郡), city (*shi*, 市), town (*chō, machi*, 町), village (*mura, son*, 村), or ward (*ku*, 区)

4. Shinmachi: destination district name

5. 1-chōme 3-2 : destination block number, section number, residence number (*chōme, banchi, gō*, 丁目, 番地, 号)

6. Nakagawa Tarō: addressee name

7. Sama: honorific suffix (*sama*, 様)

8. Tom Jones [in *katakana* script: your name]

9. Yamanashi-ken: return prefecture

10. Kitatsuru-gun: return county

11. Uenohara-machi: return village

12. Ono, return district name

13. 409-0025: return postal code

address mail from abroad using Japanese characters as long as you print "JAPAN" (in English) at the bottom of the address. An example of an envelope in Japanese is on page 84.

The Japanese post office offers all kinds of services for sending letters and packages throughout the world. Each service has its own price and requirements; inquire at the post office to see which service is the best for the package you would like to send. Below is a brief explanation of what is available.

Letters (tegami, 手紙)

Letters and business documents are divided into two groups: standard-size and nonstandard-size. Nonstandard-size mail can weigh up to 4 kg. Mini-letters (letter paper that includes an envelope and stamp) can also be purchased. These are all sent as first class mail.

Postcards (hagaki, はがき)

Prepaid postcards with a printed stamp can be purchased from the post office. An Echo-postcard (a postcard with an advertisement on it) costs ¥5 less. Reply-paid postcards (ōfuku hagaki, 往復はがき) are purchased as a set and include a return postcard. These can all be purchased at the post office or most convenience stores. All postcards are second-class mail.

Registered mail (kakitome, 書留)

This is a safe way to send important articles or cash since the entire journey is recorded. If the mail is lost, you may claim reimbursement of the amount you requested up to a maximum of ¥5,000,000 (¥500,000 for cash contents). If you are sending cash, make sure you use the proper cash registration envelope (genkin-kakitome fūtō, 現金書留封筒). You receive a registered number that lets you access an automated tracking system if your mail is lost.

Simplified registered mail (kan-i kakitome, 簡易書留)
The difference between this and registered mail is that the only things recorded are the sending and delivery.

Parcel post (Yu-Pack, kozutsumi, 小包)
Parcels up to 12 kg can be sent through parcel post. Delivery is noted with a verification postcard that is free of charge. You will receive a discount if you send more than nine parcels at one time.

Express mail (sokutatsu, 速達)
Express mail, which you should mark with a red horizontal line along the upper right portion of the address, will be given priority in delivery.

International Mail

Postcards (hagaki, はがき)
Postcards marked "Airmail" can be purchased at the post office for delivery to any destination in the world.

Letters (shojo, 書状)
Letters and documents weighing 2 kg or less can be sent anywhere in the world. Aerogrammes can also be purchased at the post office for a low price.

Printed matter (insatsubutsu, 印刷物)
Christmas cards, copied documents, books, and catalogs may be mailed at reduced rates. Write "Imprimé" or "Printed Matter" in the upper left corner on the front of the envelope or package. Packages should be given to the clerk unsealed, with the exception of books or brochures.

Small packets (kogata hōsōbutsu, 小形包装物)
You can save money when sending small and light items as "small packets." Write "Petit Paquet" or "Small Packet" in the upper left corner of the addressed side of the package. A customs label or customs declaration must also be attached. These are available at the post office.

Literature for the blind (tenji-yūbinbutsu, 点字郵便物)
Braille letters can be sent free of charge by writing "Cecogrammes" or "Literature for the Blind" in the upper right portion of the addressed side of the letter or package.

Parcel post (kozutsumi, 小包)
Parcels up to 20 kg can be sent to most destinations (for some destinations you cannot exceed 5 kg, 10 kg, or 15 kg). Proper international parcel labels such as invoices, customs declarations, and address labels are available at the post office.

Registered mail (kakitome, 書留)
By registering your package or letter, its handling from acceptance at the post office to final delivery is recorded. If your item is lost, you can obtain some amount of compensation.

Express mail (sokutatsu, 速達)
To send items by express mail, write "Express" in red ink in the upper left corner of the addressed side of the item.

Airmail (kōkūbin, 航空便)
When sending items via airmail, make sure you write "Par Avion" or "Airmail" in blue ink in the upper left corner of the addressed side of the letter or package.

EMS
EMS is the fastest and safest way of sending urgent business docu-

ments or goods overseas. EMS items are sent with acceptance receipts requiring a signature on delivery. The current whereabouts of items destined to any of twenty-one countries can be promptly traced using a computerized system. Items such as business papers, discs, merchandise samples, and any goods not specifically prohibited by the Universal Postal Convention can be sent by EMS. Valuables such as money and jewelry cannot be sent by EMS. Large quantities and sizes can be sent as a single package. Although some countries have different limits, the size limit generally is: length less then 1.5 m; length + circumference less than 3 m, and weight less then 20 kg. When sending twenty or more items, there is a 5 to 15 percent discount depending on the number of items sent. First-time users are required to complete a simple contract. In case of loss, theft, or damage, the post office will refund the value of the item up to a maximum of ¥20,000 per item. If the sender declares the value of the item in advance and pays an insurance charge of ¥50 per ¥20,000 value, the post office will refund the value of the item up to a ¥20 million maximum.

Economy Air (SAL)

SAL parcels are sent by air to overseas destinations and by surface mail within Japan. SAL is cheaper than air parcels and faster than surface parcels. SAL parcels reach Europe and North America in about three weeks and South America in three to four weeks. Make sure you attach the proper SAL sticker, which is available at the post office, to the upper left corner of the addressed side of the item. The size limit is: length less than 1.5 m, length + circumference less than 3 m, weight less than 20 kg. There is a 10 percent discount if you send ten or more items at one time and a 20 percent discount with fifty or more parcels. In case of accident, theft, damage, or loss, the post office pays an indemnity according to the weight of the item. When you send valuable items, you can insure the parcel for up to ¥2 million for a reasonable fee.

International Business Reply Service (IBRS)
IBRS allows you to send and receive postal items if you agree to pay all postage and handling charges both ways. The conditions for using this service are: (1) the minimum number of envelopes or cards in the IBRS is 100, (2) all mail must be processed within two years, (3) postage and handling charges must be paid upon delivery or by a postal-payment option, and (4) instructions should be clearly printed in black, green, or blue ink on the front of the letter or package.

International Electronic Mail (kokusai denchi yūbin, 国際電子郵便)
For businesses, conferences, and so on, information can be quickly transmitted through International Electronic Mail. Bring your message to the post office or send it from your own fax machine after completing the simple registration procedures. Documents as large as B4 size can be sent. You can use your own paper or the special A4-size sheets that are available at post offices. Messages larger than A4 size are reduced before transmission. For shorter messages, there is Mini International Electronic Mail. The standard rate of ¥1,000 applies to any destination. Special transmittal sheets are available at post offices.

Other Post Office Tips

Nondelivery notice
If you are not home when mail requiring your signature arrives, a postcard from the post office called a "Notice of Nondelivery" will be left in your mailbox. This tells you the date of the attempted delivery and contains a reply-paid postcard that you must mark and drop back in the mail. On the card you can instruct the post office to:

·   have the parcel delivered to a nearby post office

- have the package redelivered to your home on a specific date
- have the parcel delivered to a neighbor's home
- have the parcel delivered to your work place

If you would rather pick up the package at the district post office indicated on the postcard, bring the card and some form of I.D. (you will be carrying your alien registration card in any case) to the district post office where the package is being held.

Holding service and Post Restante

If you need to have your mail held for you, for example while you are out of the country, you may do so by registering at the local post office. There is also a service called "Post Restante" that delivers your mail from overseas to a designated post office where you can pick it up. Make sure you inform anyone who will mail anything to you at the designated address to write "Post Restante" above the address. You can have your mail held up to thirty days.

Change of address (tenkyo todoke, 転居届け)

If you change addresses within Japan and submit the proper change of address form to your former post office, your international and domestic mail will be forwarded to your new address for one year free of charge. If you move out of the country, only postcards and letters will be forwarded to your new overseas address, and you will be charged for any forwarded parcels.

New Year's postcards (nengajō, 年賀状)

The New Year's postcard is one of the main reasons Japanese post offices are so backed up during the New Year's season. Postcards can be sent in December and if they are marked as New Year's cards the post office will hold them for delivery on January

Sending and receiving New Year's cards is an important cultural custom in Japan; millions are delivered on January 1. If you receive a New Year's postcard from someone you did not send one to, you can redeem yourself by sending a card on the second delivery day after New Year's.

1. The Japanese New Year's postcard is a bit like the Western Christmas card. Japanese use it to thank their friends, relatives, business associates, and acquaintances for their friendship and for any favors they may have received during the year and to wish them well for the coming year. These cards can be purchased at the post office with postage prepaid, or you can buy handmade cards. The New Year's season is Japan's busiest mailing season, so you should mail your cards well in advance.

Private Services

Courier services are fast and competitively priced for sending parcels and packages within Japan. Courier parcels usually take one to two days to reach their destination and are a popular way to have ski equipment and bulky golf bags sent to vacation spots so you do not have to carry them with you on crowded trains. Courier services are available throughout Japan at convenience stores, liquor stores, and small shops. Availability is usually indicated by a long rectangular sign outside the store with the courier's company symbol. The major courier companies and their animal symbols are:

Footwork	dog
Meitetsu Transport	bear
Nippon Express	pelican

Seino Transportation	kangaroo
Yamato Transport	*kuroneko* (black cat)

Most of these services can make pickups at your office, and they will give you a better rate if your company is a regular customer. Be sure to keep the shipping form until your items have reached their destination. You can check the status of your package by calling the number on the shipping form and telling the operator your tracking number.

International courier service is also available from EMS and the following companies:

Airborne Express	(03) 5461-8412
DHL Japan	(03) 5479-2580
Federal Express	(0120) 003-200
Nippon Express	(0120) 152-259
Overseas Courier Service (OCS)	(03) 5476-8123
UPS Yamato	(0120) 271-040

EMS is the cheapest international courier service, but it has some disadvantages. The weight limit is 30 kg for the private companies, but only 20 kg with EMS. Private companies can insure any item except business documents, but EMS has only a limited level of compensation. Super-express delivery and pick up service is available from the private companies, but not with EMS.

If you are only sending documents, you can use a service called *baiku-bin* that will deliver documents anywhere in Japan in one day. Major *baiku-bin* companies are:

Baiku Kyūbin	(0120) 378-199
Business Express	(03) 3780-1111

Nihon Baiku-bin Kyōkai	(0120) 287-400
San'ei Kyūbin	(0120) 006-995
Super Express (SE)	(0120) 398-814
Tokyo Baiku-bin	(0120) 332-666

Health Matters

Most foreigners residing in Japan do not learn about Japanese hospitals or health facilities until they need them. This is fine if you do not mind the headache of learning what you need to do, where you need to go, and what you need to bring to a hospital once you feel horribly sick. But you can avoid needless hassles and wasted time if you have a general idea of how the Japanese health system works and what you need to demonstrate proof of insurance coverage. Japanese hospitals and health standards are among the best in the world, and new technologies and techniques come into use every year.

Health Insurance

After settling in, one of the first things you should do is purchase health insurance. Every foreigner who resides in Japan for more than one year is required to purchase National Health Insurance (Kokumin Kenkō Hoken, 国民健康保険), unless he or she is covered by an employee's health insurance plan or by a private health insurance plan. Those who are enrolled in a life insurance program that includes medical coverage, a travel insurance program, or a foreign student insurance program are not exempt from this requirement.

National Health Insurance (NHI) is for anyone not covered by an employee's health insurance plan or by a private insurance plan. Short-term residents, those on tourist visas, and those who have not completed their alien registration requirements are not eligible for NHI. To enroll in NHI, go to your local municipal office with your alien registration card and register at the Kokumin Kenkō Hoken section. Once you join the NHI program you will not be allowed to withdraw unless you lose eligibility, leave Japan, or join a private insurance plan. You will be issued an insurance card or certificate (*kenkō hokensho*, 健康保検証) that easily fits into a wallet. You must present this card when you receive treatment. The plan will cover 70 percent of your medical expenses. If you forget to bring your card, you will be required to pay all of the expenses and you will be reimbursed for the coverage upon presentation of the card at a later date.

Most local municipal offices have pamphlets in English explaining the whole NHI system, costs, and coverage. You are required to inform your local municipal office when:

- you join and quit the program (for example, when you switch to another company or permanently move out of the country)
- a baby is born into your family
- someone in your family dies
- your address or the head of the household changes
- you become seventy years old and you are receiving medical treatment as a retired person
- you lose your insurance card

Foreign students in Japan are required to join the NHI program. The Association of International Education Japan will pay 80 percent of the costs; the student pays the rest. Most universities will give you the appropriate materials for joining or will automatically charge you the fee.

> *If you pay into an insurance program for at least six months you will receive a partial refund upon your departure from Japan. You can obtain the Lump Sum Withdrawal Payment claim form from the Social Insurance Agency at 3-5-24 Takaido-Nishi, Suginami-ku, Tokyo 168-0071, Tel (03) 3503-1711*

Specifics of an employee's health insurance plan vary according to the industry, but premiums are based on the employee's income. You can pay the premiums (usually quarterly) at your bank, post office, or the local municipal office. You can also arrange for premiums to be automatically deducted from your bank account. Under employee health insurance plans, you must enroll in a national pension plan. Speak with your employer about the details of enrollment.

If you have a high income, it may be more economical to enroll in a private plan, since insurance fees for NHI are income based. Most U.S. insurance companies such as Blue Cross/Blue Shield and AIU provide coverage in Japan, except you are required to pay the medical fees yourself and then receive reimbursement from your insurance company upon filing a claim. Contact any of the following companies for details.

AIU Insurance	(03) 3284-4111
Alico Japan	(03) 3238-0111
Kiuchi International	(03) 3235-4010
Medicare	(0120) 634-419

Japanese Hospitals

Soon after settling into your new home, one of the first things you should do is find a local hospital that can fulfill your needs.

Although most Japanese doctors are competent in English, some smaller hospitals may be reluctant to take a foreigner who does not speak Japanese. In case of an emergency, call an ambulance by dialing 119 and tell the operator your address. The operators are trained to take addresses in English, so if you do not speak Japanese, you can speak in English, but make sure you speak slowly and with your best pronunciation.

Japan has some of the best medical resources and doctors in the world, but there are a few problems caused by inefficient management and a tendency to overprescribe medicine (especially antibiotics). It is not unusual to be prescribed ten to twenty pills a day for a common cold. One major difference between Japanese hospitals and foreign hospitals is that Japanese hospitals operate on a closed system, meaning only doctors on a particular hospital's staff are allowed to practice in that hospital. If you want the same doctor every visit, you must go to the same hospital.

There are basically two kinds of hospitals in Japan: large hospitals that are usually located in the center of a city with many doctors and nurses and that treat more serious cases, and smaller private clinics that are found in local residential areas and handle family health care. Large hospitals are often overcrowded, requiring patients to spend a long time waiting before they can see a doctor. You cannot make an appointment, and when you finally do see a doctor, the examination may be rushed in order to serve all of the waiting patients. Smaller private clinics, on the other hand, are more personal and may be more efficient, but might lack the facilities for more specialized cases.

Whenever going to a hospital, always bring your health insurance card and cash. The first place you should go to is the reception desk (*uketsuke*, 受け付), where you'll present your insurance card and explain your problem. The receptionist will then register you and guide you to the area where you wait until your name is called for your examination. Prescriptions can be filled at most large hospitals at an on-site pharmacy, but you may be required to pay at the accounts window before actually receiving the medicine. After receiving your bill, go to the accounts window and pay the balance.

Other Health Facilities

Public health centers (*hokenjo*, 保険所) are located throughout Japan in residential areas. The health centers are completely independent of hospitals. They usually offer consultation for free, and their tests are relatively inexpensive. They do not provide treatment, but they do offer tests for cancer, venereal diseases, and tuberculosis along with immunizations for polio, measles, mumps, rubella, diphtheria, whooping cough, tetanus, influenza, and meningitis. You can also get an AIDS test for a minimal price. Most health centers do not have an English-speaking staff, so if you are not confident with your Japanese, you should have a Japanese-speaking friend come with you.

Health handbooks (*kenkō techō*, 健康手帳) are issued free of charge to people forty years or older to help them keep records of their health and physical condition. If you are forty to sixty-five years of age, you can obtain this book at public health centers or medical facilities designated as health checkup facilities for adults and the elderly. Individuals sixty-five to sixty-nine years of age can obtain this book at the local welfare section of municipal offices; those seventy years and older can get it at the National Health Insurance section at the local municipal office.

Individuals from forty to sixty-four years of age are eligible for one free checkup per year at a public health center or city medical facility. Those sixty-five and older can get free health checkups twice a year. Senior citizens aged sixty-five and older are issued a health book, the *Guide to a Long Life* (*Chōju no Shiori*, 長寿のしおり), that carries a free health checkup card and information about living requirements for the elderly.

Anyone aged fifteen or older is eligible for a free tuberculosis test. Vehicles equipped with x-ray equipment tour residential areas regularly and also offer free blood pressure and urine tests. Schedules for these vehicles' visits to your neighborhood can be obtained at the local public health center. Benefits are also provided for those diagnosed with tuberculosis or venereal diseases. All this information can be found at health centers.

Dental Care

Most dental work is covered by health insurance in Japan, but you should heed the warning that although there are good dentists who practice in Japan, there are also many horrible dentists who do unnecessary procedures and use uncommon techniques. If at all possible, keep your dentist in your home country and get your check-up on your trips home. If you are going to be in Japan for a long time, do research on the dentists in your area and find out which ones other foreigners use. Japanese dentists prefer not to use anesthesia if they don't have to. Orthodontia work is not covered by insurance since having straight teeth is considered more of an aesthetic issue than a health issue. Orthodontists can be found throughout Japan but are quite expensive. Most Japanese dentists speak some English.

Prescriptions

Generally speaking, foreign prescriptions are not honored in Japan. If you are on a prescribed medicine, bring at least a six-month supply from your home country to hold you over until you can get a local doctor or pharmacy to cater to you. Bring your prescription to an English-speaking doctor who can write you a new prescription or find an appropriate substitute.

Birth Control

Until recently, birth control pills were not readily available in Japan. Because foreign prescriptions are not honored in Japan, if you are taking birth control pills you will have to make an appointment with a doctor in Japan to get a new prescription. Bring a six- to twelve-month supply with you to allow ample time to get the Japanese prescription.

There are several other kinds of contraception available in Japan such as condoms, spermicidal jellies or foams, and diaphragms. Condoms are the most common form of birth control and can be purchased at some convenience stores and at any drug store. Many pharmacies offer discreet, twenty-four-hour condom vending machines right outside the store.

Abortion

Japan has some of the most liberal abortion laws in the world and, correspondingly, some of the highest abortion rates among industrialized countries. According to Japanese law, abortions can be performed in the following cases:

- when the pregnancy has a physically or financially negative effect on the mother

- when the mother is impregnated against her will

- when either parent or immediate relative has a history of hereditary illness or psychiatric disorder.

If you would like to learn more about Japanese abortion laws or procedures contact the local obstetrics center (*sanfujinka*, 産婦人科).

Pregnancy

If you plan to have a baby in Japan, the first thing you should do is contact the local municipal office and register the pregnancy by filling out a form called the *ninshin todoke* (妊娠届). Upon completing the registration, you will be given the *Mother and Child Health Handbook* (*Boshi Kenkō Techō*, 母子健康手帳). An English version of the handbook is available from the Japanese Organization for International Cooperation in Family Planning at:

Hoken Kaikan Bekkan
1-1 Sadohara-chō, Ichigaya, Shinjuku-ku, Tokyo 162-0842
(03) 3268-5875

Bring the handbook and your health insurance card each time you go in for a checkup. The doctors will use the handbook to keep an ongoing record of the health of mother and baby. Birth takes place at a hospital, a private clinic, or (the most common choice) a specialized maternity hospital. Recently, more hospitals have begun utilizing the Lamaze method of delivery. Inquire at your hospital as soon as possible if you are interested in a Lamaze birth. Birth preparation classes are available in English from the Tokyo Childbirth Education Association (TCEA; 03-3440-1657) and the Aiku Maternal and Child Care Center (03-3473-8312). Home births are neither common nor recommended.

You may be entitled to various forms of assistance and aid after receiving the *Mother and Child Health Handbook*. If you send the birth announcement card to the health center you are entitled to free visits from a public health nurse. This service is only available for your first baby.

The delivery will not be fully covered by the insurance company, since pregnancy is not considered an illness except in certain circumstances, such as when there are complications. However, it's good to check with your local city office to see if you are eligible for full or partial reimbursement of the delivery costs.

Using the coupons in the *Mother and Child Health Handbook* you can receive a free hepatitis B check and free vaccinations for the infant. The following chart shows the vaccinations and periods of inoculation required by Japanese health standards:

TYPE OF VACCINATION	TIME FROM BIRTH
influenza	from 3 years old, for nursery school, kindergarten, primary, and junior high school (twice a year)
polio	3–48 months (twice)
BCG	0–48 months, the first year of primary school and the first year of junior high school
whooping cough, diphtheria, and tetanus	· first period 3–48 months (three times) · second period 12–18 months (after the first period is over) · third period the 6th year of primary school
measles	12–72 months
general measles	the first year, the third year of junior high school (girls only)
Japanese encephalitis	· first vaccination at 3 years of age (twice) · second vaccination the following year (once)

If one of the parents is a Japanese citizen, the baby's birth must be reported within fourteen days (three months if the baby

Many non-Japanese have gone to Japan as youths and spent the rest of their lives there. Some went to Japan to get away, but most went because they were attracted to the culture or fell in love with a citizen and just ended up staying. Many children of such international marriages from the 1960s and 1970s are contributing greatly to Japan's continuing process of globalization.

was born outside of Japan) by either a parent, a person living with the child, the doctor, or a midwife who was present at the birth. Register at the Family Registration Section (Koseki Gakari, 戸籍 係り) of the municipal office for the mother's residence, the residence of the person who files the report, or the place the baby was born. Bring one copy of the "Certificate of Completion of Birth Report" (*Shussei Todoke*, 出生届) and the *Mother and Child Health Handbook*. The birth must also be reported to the embassy or consulate of the home country of the foreign national as well.

If both parents are foreign nationals and the baby will be in Japan for at least sixty days from the date of birth, the birth must be reported the same way as above. Also, the baby's alien registration must be reported at the local municipal office. For details on this procedure see "Permission to Acquire Residency Status" in the chapter "Immigration Procedures."

To receive a passport for the baby, go to the embassy or consulate general's office for the home country of the non-Japanese parent and get the proper documents and registration forms. You must also get the baby's residential permit. This must be done through the Immigration Bureau within thirty days of the date of birth. Details are outlined in the chapter "Immigration Procedures." Both the baby's passport and alien registration certificate must be brought to the Alien Registration section for inspection within fourteen days of receiving the certificate. For questions or details call the Civil Affairs Department, Nationality Section, at (03) 3214-6231, ext. 2350.

Medical Vocabulary

Should you ever find yourself in need of medical attention and need to communicate your symptoms in Japanese, the following list of words in English, romanized Japanese, and Japanese *kanji* characters may come in handy.

BODY PARTS

appendix	*mōchō*	盲腸
arm	*ude*	腕
armpit	*waki no shita*	わきの下
artery	*dōmyaku*	動脈
back	*senaka*	背中
bladder	*bōkō*	ぼうこう
blood	*chi*	血
blood vessel	*kekkan*	血管
bone	*hone*	骨
buttocks	*shiri*	尻
cheek	*hoho*	頬
chest, bust	*mune*	胸
chin	*ago*	顎
ear	*mimi*	耳
elbow	*hiji*	肘
eye	*me*	目
eyebrow	*mayuge*	眉毛
eyelash	*matsuge*	まつげ
face	*kao*	顔

finger	*yubi*	指
forehead	*hitai*	額
hair	*kaminoke*	髪の毛
hand	*te*	手
head	*atama*	頭
heart	*shinzō*	心臓
kidney	*jinzō*	腎臓
knee	*hiza*	膝
liver	*kanzō*	肝臓
lung	*hai*	肺
mouth	*kuchi*	口
muscle	*kinniku*	筋肉
navel	*heso*	へそ
neck	*kubi*	首
nose	*hana*	鼻
pancreas	*suizō*	膵臓
shoulder	*kata*	肩
stomach	*onaka*	お腹
throat	*nodo*	のど
toe	*ashi no yubi*	足の指
tongue	*shita*	舌
tooth	*ha*	歯
windpipe	*kikan*	気管

DESCRIBING YOUR CONDITION

be in a haze	*bonyari shite iru*	ぼんやりしている
faint	*shisshin*	失神
fatigue	*hirō*	疲労
shiver	*furueru*	震える
chill	*samuke*	寒気
headache	*zutsū*	頭痛
sweat	*hakkan*	発汗
sleepy	*nemui*	眠い
weary	*darui*	だるい

USEFUL PHRASES

My (_____) hurts

Watashi no (_____) ga itai desu
私の（＿＿）が痛いです

My (_____) itches

Watashi no (_____) ga kayui desu
私の(＿＿)が痒いです

I have a fever

Netsu ga arimasu
熱があります

I have a cold

Kaze o hiita yō desu
風邪をひいたようです

I feel sick (to my stomach)

(Onaka no chōshi) ga warui desu

お腹の調子が悪いです

I have diarrhea

Geri o shite imasu

下痢をしています

I threw up

Haite shimaimashita

吐いてしまいました

COMMON ILLNESSES AND CONDITIONS

anemia	*hinketsu*	貧血
appendicitis	*mōchōen*	盲腸炎
asthma	*zensoku*	喘息
abdominal pain	*fukutsū*	腹痛
allergy	*arerugii*	アレルギー
backache	*senaka no itami*	背中の痛み
bloody stool	*ketsuben*	血便
bronchitis	*kikanshien*	気管支炎
cancer	*gan*	癌
chest pain	*mune no itami*	胸の痛み
cold	*kaze*	風邪
constipation	*benpi*	便秘
cough	*seki ga deru*	咳が出る
diabetes	*tōnyōbyō*	糖尿病
diarrhea	*geri*	下痢

difficulty in breathing	*kokyū konnan*	呼吸困難
food poisoning	*shoku chūdoku*	食中毒
gastritis	*i-en*	胃炎
getting tired easily	*tsukareyasui*	疲れやすい
heart attack	*shinzō mahi*	心臓麻痺
heartburn	*muneyake*	胸やけ
hemorrhoids	*ji*	痔
hernia	*herunia*	ヘルニア
high blood pressure	*kōketsuatsu*	高血圧
hives	*jinmashin*	じんましん
insomnia	*fuminshō*	不眠症
irregular pulse	*myaku ga midareru*	脈が乱れる
loss of strength	*datsuryoku kan*	脱力感
low blood pressure	*teiketsuatsu*	低血圧
nose bleed	*hanaji*	鼻血
measles	*hashika*	はしか
miscarriage	*ryūsan*	流産
palpitation	*dōki*	どうき
pneumonia	*haien*	肺炎
rapid heart action	*myaku ga hayai*	脈がはやい
slow heart rate	*myaku ga sukunai*	脈が少ない
sore throat	*nodo no itami*	喉の痛み
stomach ache	*i-tsū*	胃痛
stroke	*nōikketsu*	脳溢血
tonsils	*hentōsen*	へんとうせん

ulcer	*kaiyō*	潰瘍
vomit blood	*chi o haku*	血を吐く

OTHER USEFUL WORDS

ambulance	*kyūkyūsha*	救急車
antibiotics	*kōsei busshitsu*	抗生物質
antiseptics	*shōdokuzai*	消毒剤
bandage	*hōtai*	包帯
bowel movement	*bentsū*	便通
blood pressure	*ketsuatsu*	血圧
digestive aid	*shōkazai*	消化剤
eyedrops	*megusuri*	目薬
examination	*shinsatsu*	診察
hospital	*byōin*	病院
medicine	*kusuri*	薬
nurse	*kangofu*	看護婦
pain reliever	*itamidome*	痛み止め
pharmacy	*yakkyoku*	薬局
prescription	*shohōsen*	処方箋
sleeping pill	*suiminyaku*	睡眠薬
suppository	*zayaku*	座薬
symptom	*shōjō*	症状
thermometer	*taionkei*	体温計
x-ray	*rentogen*	レントゲン

HOSPITAL DEPARTMENTS

Anesthesiology	*masuika*	麻酔科
Dentistry	*shika*	歯科
Dermatology	*hifuka*	皮膚科
Ear, Nose, and Throat	*jibiinkōka*	耳鼻咽喉科
Ophthalmology	*ganka*	眼科
Internal Medicines	*naika*	内科
Obstetrics and Gynecology	*sanfujinka*	産婦人科
Orthopedics	*seikeigeka*	整形外科
Pediatrics	*shōnika*	小児科
Psychiatry	*seishin shinkeika*	精神神経科
Surgery	*geka*	外科
Urology	*hinyōkika*	泌尿器科

VOCABULARY BY MEDICAL SPECIALTY

Dentistry

bad breath	*kōshū*	口臭
bleeding gums	*haguki kara chi ga deru*	歯ぐきから血が出る
cavity	*mushiba*	虫歯
crown	*shikan*	歯冠
denture	*ireba*	入れ歯
filling	*tsumemono*	詰め物
gums	*haguki*	歯ぐき

loose tooth	*ha ga guragura suru*	歯がぐらぐらする
lose a tooth	*ha ga nukeru*	歯が抜ける
nerve	*shinkei*	神経
plaque	*shikō*	歯垢
pull a tooth	*ha o nuku*	歯を抜く
sore in the mouth	*kōnaien*	口内炎
swollen gums	*haguki ga hareteiru*	歯ぐきが腫れている
toothache	*haita*	歯痛
wisdom teeth	*oyashirazu*	親知らず

Dermatology

allergy	*arerugii*	アレルギー
athlete's foot	*mizumushi*	水虫
bee sting	*hachisasare*	蜂刺され
blister	*mizubukure*	水膨れ
bruise	*murasaki no hantan*	紫の斑点
burn	*yakedo*	火傷
dry skin	*kansō hada*	乾燥肌
eczema	*shisshin*	湿疹
falling hair	*datsumō*	脱毛
hives	*jinmashin*	じんましん
itchy	*kayui*	かゆい
minute hemorrhagic spot	*shukketsu han*	出血斑

pus	*umi*	うみ
red rash	*akai hanten*	赤い斑点
skin eruption rash	*fukidemono*	吹き出物
skin rash	*kabure*	かぶれ

Ear, Nose, and Throat

can't distinguish smells	*hana ga kikanai*	鼻がきかない
sense of taste changes	*aji ga hen ni kanjiru*	味が変に感じる
difficulty in hearing	*chōryoku teika*	聴力低下
ear discharge	*mimidare*	耳だれ
earache	*mimi ga itai*	耳が痛い
eardrum	*komaku*	鼓膜
hoarse throat	*nodo ga zeizei suru*	喉がぜいぜいする
hoarse voice	*koe ga kareru*	声がかれる
loss of voice	*koe ga denai*	声がでない
nosebleed	*hanaji*	鼻血
ringing in the ear	*miminari*	耳鳴り
runny nose	*hanamizu*	鼻水
sneeze	*kushami*	くしゃみ
snore	*ibiki*	いびき
stuffy nose	*hana ga tsumaru*	鼻がつまる

Neurology

coma	*konsui*	昏眠

convulsion	*keiren*	けいれん
delirium	*uwagoto*	うわ言
drowsy	*utō to shita jōtai*	うとうととした状態
epilepsy	*tenkan*	てんかん
hallucination	*genkaku*	幻覚
joint pain	*kansetsutsū*	関節痛
migraine	*henzutsū*	編頭痛
muscular pain	*kinnikutsū*	筋肉痛
numbness	*kankaku mahi*	感覚麻痺
paralysis	*shishi no mahi*	四肢の麻痺
seizure	*hossa*	発作
sleepy	*nemui*	眠い
speech disturbance	*gengo shōgai*	言語障害
tremor	*tesaki ga furueru*	手先が震える
visual disturbance	*shiryoku gentai*	視力減退

Obstetrics and Gynecology

abdomen	*hara*	腹
breast	*mune*	胸
delivery	*bunben*	分娩
Fallopian tube	*rankan*	卵管
hemorrhage	*fusei shukketsu*	不正出血
labor	*jintsū*	陣痛
lower abdominal pain	*kafukubutsū*	下腹部痛
menopausal	*mu gekkei*	無月経

menstruation	seiri	生理
morning sickness	tsuwari	つわり
ovary	ransō	卵巣
ovum	ranshi	卵子
pregnancy	ninshin	妊娠
reproductive organs	seiki	性器
uterus	shikyū	子宮
vagina	chitsu	ちつ
vaginal discharge	orimono	おりもの
venereal disease	seibyō	性病

Ophthalmology

astigmatism	ranshi	乱視
blurred vision	me ga kasumu	目がかすむ
color blindness	shikimō	色盲
conjunctivitis	ketsumakuen	結膜炎
eye discharge	meyani	目やに
eyeball	gankyū	眼球
eyestrain	me no hirō	目の疲労
farsighted	enshi	遠視
foreign matter in the eye	me no gomi	目のごみ
nearsighted	kinshi	近視
poor vision	shiryoku teika	視力低下
red eye	jūketsu	充血
squint	shashi	斜視

sty	*monomorai*	ものもらい
visual disturbance	*shiryoku shōgai*	視力障害

Pediatrics

chickenpox	*mizu bōsō*	水ぼうそう
convulsions	*keiren*	けいれん
measles	*hashika*	はしか
irritability	*muzukaru*	むずかる

Surgery

bruise	*daboku*	打撲
cast	*gibusu*	ギブス
cut	*kirikizu*	切り傷
dislocation	*dakkyū*	脱臼
external injury	*gaishō*	外傷
fracture	*kossetsu*	骨折
internal bleeding	*nai shukketsu*	内出血
lower back pain	*koshi ga itamu*	腰が痛む
numb	*shibireru*	しびれる
slipped disk	*gikkuri goshi*	ぎっくり腰
sprain	*nenza suru*	捻挫する
sprained finger	*tsukiyubi suru*	突き指する
stab	*sashi kizu*	刺し傷
swollen	*hareteiru*	はれている

Urology

bladder	*bōsō*	ぼうこう
blood in urine	*ketsunyō*	血尿
difficulty in urinating	*shōben ga denikui*	小便がでにくい
discolored urine	*nigotta nyō*	濁った尿
frequent urge to urinate	*shōben ga chikai*	小便が近い
gonorrhea	*rinbyō*	淋病
painful urination	*shōben no toki itai*	小便の時痛い
pus in urine	*nōnyō*	濃尿
urinary incontinence	*shikkin*	失禁

Finding a School
and Finding a Job

Despite its complicated writing system, Japan has an extremely high literacy rate. Japanese children study *kanji* characters from elementary school until they get into college. Children start preschool between the ages of three and six. Preschool is followed by the 6-3-3-4 system: six years of elementary school, three years of junior high, three years of high school, and four years of college.

For Japanese citizens, elementary school and junior high school are mandatory. The local board of education sends a school enrollment notice (*shūgaku annai*, 就学案内) to parents and guardians in mid-October for elementary school students and at the beginning of November for junior high school students.

Japanese students compete at an early age to get into top schools in their areas. When entering high school, junior high school, or even elementary school, students take rigorous tests.

The steps that will lead into the best universities generally begin at the preschool level. After the students' long hours of daily study at school, most will go to cram schools (*juku*,

塾) in the evening to get an extra edge. There is tremendous pressure on students to do well on their entrance examinations (*juken*, 受験). The extremely stressful academic environment produces a highly educated country, but it is also a factor in Japan having a very high teenage suicide rate.

Schools for Foreign Children

International Schools

Many foreign families residing in Japan send their children to international schools. International schools are located throughout Japan, with the majority n big cities like Tokyo and Osaka. There are also American, Canadian, and British schools that comply with the educational standards of those countries. You need not be a citizen of that country to attend these schools; many students are, in fact, Japanese children with some schooling abroad or whose parents are interested in international schooling. The quality of education in international schools is generally high, and children graduating from these schools are often fluent in two or three languages. See "Important Phone Numbers and Addresses" at the back of this book to find schools in your area.

Japanese Schools

Foreign students are permitted to attend Japanese schools. If you wish to send your child to a Japanese school, you must apply at the local board of education by presenting the child's alien registration card. The board of education will require the child to have a physical examination before entering at the elementary level. If the child is beyond elementary school level, visit the school entrance section at the local city hall.

Attending a Japanese school for a foreign child has both good and bad aspects. It takes a while before a foreign child's language ability is equal to that of his or her peers. This can be lonely and very frustrating for a child. In addition, other children may be cruel to a foreign student. One of the biggest problems in modern Japanese schools is bullying (ijime, 苛め). Japan is a homogeneous country where anything out of the ordinary or individualistic is generally frowned upon. A foreign student, especially at a young age, may be the target of teasing and taunting.

On the other hand, if a foreign student goes through the Japanese educational system, he or she will be fluent in Japanese. The younger a child starts learning Japanese the easier it will be to master. In the last ten years, as the foreign population in Japan has increased, it is more common to see a young foreign child speaking fluent Japanese. This language skill can have tremendous advantages for getting into good universities in both Japan and abroad.

Higher Education in Japan

There are now more international students in Japan than at any other time in Japanese history. In 1975, there were just over ten thousand international students studying in Japan. By 1995, this number had surpassed eighty-five thousand. The Japanese Ministry of Education has an ambitious goal to continue the upward trend. The Japanese government is actively encouraging foreigners to study in Japan and has taken measures together with the AIEJ (Association of International Education, Japan; see below) to make information and funds more accessible.

There are five different types of institutions of higher education in Japan: universities, graduate schools, junior colleges, special training colleges, and colleges of technology.

Universities (daigaku, 大学)

Universities provide four-year academic programs (six years for medicine, dentistry, and veterinary science). An international student can attend a university under three different statuses:

1. **Full-time**. A program of study for full-time students at universities lasts four years. This is not recommended for a student who will be in Japan for only a couple of years but rather for the student who wishes to receive a degree from a Japanese university.

2. **Auditors**. As an auditor, you do not earn college credit for completed courses, and universities may have restrictions on courses that are open to you. This option may be good for students who want to further their education but do not need college credits. Additionally, an auditor does not have to go through the normal admission process.

3. **Part-time students**. The conditions for part-time study are almost the same as for auditors except that credits are given for completed courses.

Graduate schools (daigakuin, 大学院)

A student may enter graduate school after the successful completion of a four-year undergraduate program. Japanese graduate schools offer master- and doctoral-level courses, with the length of study depending on the field. Some universities also accept postgraduate research students, auditors, and part-time students. A student may attend a graduate school under one of the four following statuses:

1. **Full-time**. Conditions are the same as undergraduate status.

2. **Auditors**. Conditions are the same as undergraduate status.

3. **Part-time**. Conditions are the same as undergraduate status.

4. **Research** (*kenkyūsei*, 研究生). Qualifications depend on the university. This may be good for students interested in engaging in research in special fields without the goal of acquiring credits. Length of study is generally one semester to one year.

Junior colleges (tandai, 短大)
The length of study at a junior college is usually two years. About 60 percent of Japan's junior colleges are for women only. They generally offer courses in home economics, foreign languages, literature, education, and health and welfare.

Special training colleges (senmongakkō, 専門学校)
Special training colleges offer vocational training programs that can last anywhere from one to three years.

Technology colleges (kōtō senmongakkō, 高等専門学校)
Technology colleges are for junior high school graduates who are mechanically or technically inclined. The period of study is five years. Most schools offer courses in science, engineering, merchant shipping, and other similar fields. Most foreigners cannot attend this kind of school since admission is determined upon completion of junior high school in Japan.

Japanese-Language Institutes

If your goal is simply to study Japanese, the best school for you may be a Japanese-language institute. Japanese-language institutes are schools accredited by the Association for the Promotion of Japanese-Language Education or are run by private universities as preparatory Japanese-language programs. There are over 1,600 Japanese-language schools scattered throughout the country. These programs are intended for students who wish to study Japanese language, culture, or basic subjects for a university entrance examination. Most students at these schools are international students who plan to attend Japanese universities, foreign technical trainees, and foreign residents and their children. The term of study is anywhere from six months to one year. To find listings of accredited schools in your area, check with the AIEJ (see below). For a list of schools that offer programs in learning Japanese, see the section "Important Phone Numbers and Addresses" at the back of this book.

To obtain a student visa for a language institution, the student usually must have completed twelve years of school in his or her home country. The following documents are required:

- application form

- high school or college transcript

- certificate of study

- letter of recommendation

- certificate of financial capability

- medical certificate

- guarantor-related documents

- application fee (usually about ¥30,000)

One- and two-year courses usually begin in April, and eighteen-month courses in October. Applicants should apply six to eight months before the term begins to allow ample time for application procedures.

There are two important points to keep in mind when choosing a language school:

1. Before it can grant a student visa, the school must be accredited by the Association for the Promotion of Japanese-Language Education. Check the publication "Japanese Language Institutes of Japan," which can be obtained from the Association of International Education office, libraries in Japan, and Japanese embassies and consulates, to see which institutes are accredited.

2. Once you enter Japan, you are not allowed to transfer from one language institute to another or from a language institute to a preparatory Japanese-language program at a private university without leaving the country and applying for a new visa.

Choosing a School

There are many factors to be taken into account when choosing which school you want to attend. Japan has thousands of schools, all of them different; it may be difficult to find the school that is best for you. Consider the following factors:

- whether the school is accredited by the Association for the Promotion of Japanese-Language Education

- how long you will be in Japan

- your present level of ability in Japanese

- expenses vs. your funds and financial aid resources

- course content, both Japanese courses and special programs for international students

- the school's location

Length of Stay

The first thing to consider when choosing a school is the duration of your stay in Japan. The longer you will be in Japan the more options you have. There are universities and language institutes that offer programs for short-term international students. These can last anywhere from a month to a year. Visa requirements vary depending on your nationality, so check with the Japanese embassy or consulate general's office in your country before coming to Japan. Most of these programs are Japanese-language programs, exchange programs, or research student programs.

A handful of universities are very popular with international students. Most of these universities have an international department (*kokusaibu*, 国際部) that offers courses in English. Some universities have summer programs and one-year programs for foreigners wishing to study Japanese. Most credits for these courses should be transferrable. Check with your home university to make sure the credits will be recognized before you go to Japan. Admission requirements vary from university to university. Refer to the listings in the section "Important Phone Numbers and Addresses" at the back of this book for universities with special programs for international students.

Long-term study is considered to be two years or more. International students who wish to graduate from a Japanese university or institute are long-term students. The admission standards for long-term students are generally much more stringent than those for short-term students. At most universities the student will have to pass the top level of the Japanese Proficiency Examination and the entrance examination for foreign students. The openings for foreign students are limited, so admissions can be very competitive. If there is no special examination for foreign students the student will have to pass the same exam that Japanese students take.

All the schools listed at the back of this book have special programs for international students, but many have special entrance examinations for foreign students (*ryūgakusei*, 留学生) and special examinations for Japanese who grew up abroad and did not receive a Japanese education (*kikokushijo*, 帰国子女). Check with the particular university you are interested in for admission requirements for international students. It is also a good idea to check the level of Japanese proficiency of the other international students and the percentage of students from China and Taiwan (Chinese students tend to have an advantage learning Japanese since they already know the *kanji* characters) to see if your Japanese-language abilities are sufficient.

Language Capability

Each school will have different admission requirements for international students. If the school is a language institute, there will most likely be all levels of Japanese language offered. If the school is a university or is primarily designed for Japanese students, there may be few useful language courses offered. Some universities have no Japanese-language requirements if you speak English. Some universities require foreign students to sit for their regular (Japanese) entrance examination. Other universities base admissions on the results of the Japanese Language Proficiency Examination (Nihongo Nōryoku Shiken, 日本語能力試験) and the General Examination for Foreign Students. If you have not passed level one of the Japanese Language Proficiency Examination, it would be a good idea to find out the percentage of international students at the school you are interested in who scored above 200 on level one (indicating an excellent level of fluency). Consider improving your Japanese until you are up to the level of the international students who will be your classmates, or finding a school that is more in line with your abilities.

Expenses and Financial Aid Resources

Japan is one of the most expensive places in the world to live, and this can be a big obstacle for foreign students, who must pay for rent and food as well as tuition. To be eligible for a student visa, you have to provide proof that you have the means to fund your schooling. Some international students work part-time jobs to help finance their stay in Japan. If English is your native language, you could consider tutoring English. Some English tutoring jobs pay very well. Be aware that under the student visa status you are only allowed to work up to twenty-eight hours per week and up to eight hours per day during long vacation periods. Research students are only allowed to work up to fourteen hours per week and up to eight hours per day during long vacation periods. Precollege students in Japanese-language institutes are only allowed to work up to four hours per day.

Scholarships are available to international students. Most of these are available to students only after they have come to Japan, but some scholarship applications—such as those from the Japanese Ministry of Education (Monbushō, 文部省)—are accepted before arrival (check with the Japanese embassy or consulate general's office in your home country). Scholarships are also offered from local governments, international institutions, and private companies for students who live or attend schools in their district; these scholarships vary as to eligibility and stipends. Several private foundations also offer scholarships; these are usually sponsored by companies or organizations with a common objective or interest in a particular student. Some schools also offer scholarships directly to their students. Inquire with the school you want to attend for information and prerequisites. The AIEJ publishes a guide in Japanese, English, and Korean called "Scholarships for International Students in Japan" that lists hundreds of scholarships and is an excellent resource for students.

The AIEJ has made tuition fee waiving arrangements with private colleges, graduate schools, and junior colleges: up to 30 percent of the tuition can be waived for privately financed international students. There are also arrangements for tuition reductions for students of national and local public universities. For more information refer to the pamphlet "Privately Financed Foreign Students Guide to College Admission" (Shihi Gaikokujin Ryūgakusei no Tame no Daigaku Nyūgaku Annai, 私費外国人留学生のための大学入学案内). This Japanese-language publication can be obtained from the AIEJ.

Course Content

When investigating a study program, check to see how long it has been in operation as well as the course content. If a course has only been available for a couple of years, chances are that it will still have problems and may not be as good as an older program. Also, if possible, speak to students who have already attended the school to get their opinion. Always examine several universities since you may not be admitted to your first-choice school. To obtain information on each university's examination dates and subjects covered, refer to the "Privately Financed Foreign Students Guide to College Admission."

Location

Most international students study in the Tokyo (Kantō) area, where most of the schools with established international programs are located. But there are several advantages to considering universities outside the Kantō region. Other regions offer lower tuition and a lower cost of living. There are more opportunities to get to know the local community in smaller cities. Finally, for a student of the Japanese language, a countryside setting is a better environment to study the language, since Tokyo is full of foreigners as well as Japanese who can speak English.

AIEJ
Association of International Education, Japan

日本国際教育協会留学情報センター

Nihon Kokusai Kyōiku Kyōkai Ryūgaku Jōhō Sentaa

The Association of International Education is an organization that provides information about studying in Japan to international students and information about studying abroad to Japanese students. It is an excellent resource with which to begin. The AIEJ provides several services to foreigners who wish to study in Japan:

- affordable housing at the center for qualified international students. Inquire at the center

- a reference library with books, pamphlets, videos, and information on universities, special training colleges, and language school programs

- counseling services and advice for students about universities and language institutes

- Japan Education Fairs in Asian countries, Europe, Australia, and the United States

- Education Fairs in Tokyo and Osaka

- publications such as "The Student Guide to Japan," "Scholarships for International Students in Japan," "Index of Majors," and "Japanese Colleges and Universities"

- a website with updated information at www.aiej.or.jp

The AIEJ has two locations in Japan and a voice and fax information service that can be used to obtain information about scholarship programs, Japanese-language institutes, universities and graduate schools, special training colleges, homestays, visas, and so on. To use the fax service, dial the information service number, choose Japanese or English, and follow the instructions:

Tokyo Center
4-5-29 Komaba, Meguro-ku, Tokyo 153-8503
Tel (03) 5454-5216, Fax (03) 5454-5236

Kobe Center
1-2-8 Wakihama-chō, Chūō-ku, Kobe-shi, Hyōgo 651-0072
Tel (078) 242-1742, Fax (078) 242-1743

Working in Japan

Finding a good job in Japan is difficult enough without the added disadvantage of being a foreigner. It is hard for a foreigner to find a job in Japan because the hiring company has to be willing to sponsor the foreigner for a work visa, and this involves extra money, effort, and time. On top of this, Japan is trying to work its way out of its deepest recession since World War II, making it difficult even for Japanese to find jobs. There is, however, demand for foreigners in certain fields—it is just a matter of finding these jobs. It helps if you can pass at least level two on the Japanese Language Proficiency Test and can speak polite Japanese, although many companies do not require it. If you switch jobs while you are in Japan, you may need to change your visa (see the chapter "Immigration Procedures"). Below are some ideas and resources to help you when you're looking for a job.

Teaching English

Teaching English is the job to find if you have no experience and come from an English-speaking country. There are many English conversation schools throughout Japan. Just inquire at the school

Got a job in Japan? Some tips for making the harried commuting life a bit less of a hassle:

- Take a new way home from the station every day. Get out of that rut!
- Ride a bike instead of taking the subway. This is especially useful if you live someplace like Tokyo. You will be amazed at how your big city shrinks (and what you'll find!) when you can see what really lies between each of those subway stops.
- If you're American, beware of friendly drunks who may turn on you, blaming you for WWII. Try not to take it personally.
- Watch your step on train platforms. "Platform Pizzas" can appear at any time of day or night, not just on weekend evenings, as you might expect.
- Find alternatives to the typical meeting places near stations. For example, Hachiko (the plaza around the bronze dog statue) in Shibuya, Tokyo, can be a complete zoo, so establish a meeting point at the easily-spotted-but-much-less-crowded coffee shop across the street.

or look for advertisements for schools that are hiring. The JET Program puts thousands of English teachers in high schools and junior high schools every year. To apply to the JET Program you must interview outside of Japan through a Japanese consulate. Contact the Japanese consulate in your home country for more information.

Monday Edition of the *Japan Times*

The Monday edition of the *Japan Times* usually has at least five pages of jobs listed in the classified section. There are all kinds of jobs advertised—from English-teaching jobs to hostess jobs to managerial positions in large companies. Most of the jobs are in the Tokyo area, but there are also some listings for the Kansai area (Kyoto–Osaka–Kobe). An online edition of the *Japan Times* also has listings.

American Chamber of Commerce Japan (ACCJ)

You can put your resume on the ACCJ's web site (www.accj.or.jp) for three months for a small fee. Hundreds of companies have access to this site and use it when looking for potential employees. You do not have to be an American citizen to use this service.

Executive Recruiting Firms

Executive recruiting firms are paid by other companies to find employees for them. The type of candidates they deal with are people with a lot of experience in a particular field or those with graduate-level degrees. Japan has many recruiting firms that can help you find a more rewarding job. Here are some of them, as compiled by the American Chamber of Commerce:

A.C.E. Japan Incorporated
Tel (03) 3503-2251, Fax (03) 3503-2254

Alex Tsukada International Ltd.
Tel (03) 3478-5477, Fax (03) 3408-6753

Asia-Net K.K.
Tel/Fax (03) 3280-0490

Axiom Co., Ltd.
Tel (03) 5294-6343, Fax (03) 5294-6344

Cambridge Research Institute, Inc.
Tel (03) 3582-8931, Fax (03) 3505-4539

CDS Consulting
Tel (03) 5457-3501, Fax (03) 5457-3502

CS Inc.
Tel (03) 5466-8585, Fax (03) 5466-8494

Dynamic Search Co., Ltd.
Tel (03) 5226-0181, Fax (03) 5226-0182

East West Consulting K.K.
Tel (03) 3222-5531, Fax (03) 3222-5535

Execnet, Inc.
Tel (03) 5443-5980, Fax (03) 5443-7533

Executive Consultants International Inc.
Tel (03) 5570-7272, Fax (03) 5570-7271

Executive Search International, Inc.
Tel (03) 3479-0918, Fax (03) 3479-0858

Heidrick and Struggles Japan Ltd.
Tel (03) 3500-5310, Fax (03) 3500-5350

Hodgson and Company
Tel (03) 3531-7522, Fax (03) 3531-7566

Honjo Associates, Certified Public Accountants
Tel (03) 5275-2262, Fax (03) 5275-2289

Human Associates, Inc.
Tel (03) 5512-6504, Fax (03) 5512-6442

IBI, Inc.
Tel (03) 3230-2151, Fax (03) 3234-6167

Institute for Social Engineering, Inc.
Tel (03) 3478-4891, Fax (03) 3402-2454

International Business Consultant, Inc.
Tel (03) 3239-4500, Fax (03) 5213-5266

International Computer Professional Associates
Tel (03) 5325-3218, Fax (03) 5325-3219

InterSearch Japan Wouters and Associates Inc.
Tel (03) 3423-7491, Fax (03) 3423-7492

JAFCO Co., Ltd.
Tel (03) 5223-7549, Fax (03) 5223-7562

Nihon Best Family Co., Ltd.
Tel (03) 3358-0700, Fax (03) 3358-0723

Oak Associates, K.K.
Tel (03) 5472-7075, Fax (03) 5472-7076

PA Consulting Group
Tel (03) 3433-3921, Fax (03) 3433-0163

Pacifica Consultants
Tel (03) 3224-0915, Fax (03) 3224-0916

Ray and Berndtson
Tel (03) 5211-8411, Fax (03) 3264-0910

RCS Inc.
Tel (03) 3863-1412, Fax (03) 3863-1413

Recruit Ablic Inc.
Tel (03) 3592-5551, Fax (03) 3592-9029

Russell Reynolds Associates Japan, Inc.
Tel (03) 3216-4336, Fax (03) 3216-5866

Signium International Co., Ltd.
Tel (03) 3239-8005, Fax (03) 3239-8283

Spencer Stuart Japan Ltd.
Tel (03) 3238-7081, Fax (03) 3238-8902

Sun Elite Corporation
Tel (03) 3639-1341, Fax (03) 3639-1509

Telesight Corporation
Tel (03) 3770-6858, Fax (03) 3770-6703

TMT Inc.
Tel (03) 3261-6471, Fax (03) 3221-0601

Tokyo Executive Search Co., Ltd.
Tel (03) 3230-1881, Fax (03) 3230-2860

Veritas International, Inc.
Tel (03) 3440-8404, Fax (03) 3440-8474

Public Transportation

Japan has roughly half the population of the U.S. packed into an area about the size of California. Unless you live in the countryside or have a lot of money to spend on the luxury of a car, you will quickly get familiar with Japan's various public transportation systems. The average suburban Japanese commutes well over an hour to work. Real estate prices near the center of the city are too high for the average family to afford, making Japan's superb transportation system not only convenient but necessary. Japan's economic boom along with the network of bullet trains (*shinkansen*, 新幹線) has even created a type of "salaryman" (office worker) called *tanshinfunin* (単身赴任). A *tanshinfunin* travels, sometimes up to halfway across the country, on bullet trains to Tokyo, Osaka, or some other big city for the weekdays and returns home to be with the family on the weekends.

The most common forms of public transportation in Japan are trains, subways, and buses. Most trains and subways start running at about 5:00 A.M. and go until 1:00 A.M. Looking at a map of a train system, especially of Tokyo, can be overwhelming. If

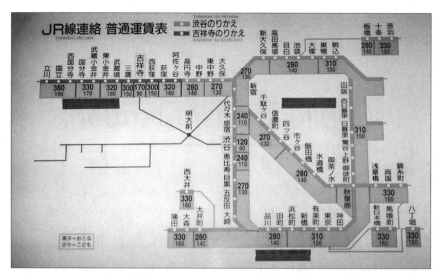

A station map showing Japan Railways fares for transfers. The smaller numbers represent children's fares. You may need to memorize the characters for your destination station, or you can buy the minimum fare and pay the difference when you arrive. Most train and subway stations in Japan also have maps with station names and routes written in romanized form.

you do not read or write Japanese, the first thing you should do is have someone write the name of your station and line on a piece of paper that you can carry with you at all times until you recognize the characters yourself. Have someone who knows the system take you to all the destinations you may need to go, such as work or school. Learn both the characters and the phonetic pronunciation for any destination station, stations where you may need to make transfers, and the lines you need to use. The names of major stations will probably be written in English, but it is a good idea to memorize the characters anyway.

Trains and Subways

To buy a ticket for a train or the subway, go to the ticket-selling area (*kippu-uriba*, 切符売り場). On or above each ticket machine will be a map. The station you are at will be highlighted in red to

> **I**f you cannot read the signs or are unsure of the price of the ticket, buy the cheapest ticket; when you get to your destination give the ticket to the person at the gate, and he will tell you the difference you have to pay. Many stations have yellow "Fare Adjustment" machines clearly marked in English. Put your ticket into this machine and insert the amount of money displayed on the screen. The machine will then spit out a new ticket that you can use to exit the station.

show your current location (*tō-eki*, 当駅). Your destination will have a number under it, which is the amount of the fare to get there. If there are two numbers listed, one in black and one in red, the red number is the price for children eleven years old or younger. To purchase a child's ticket make sure you push the button marked "Child" (こども) before pushing any other button.

When purchasing more than one ticket, push the button marked for two tickets (*ni-mai*, 二枚) or three tickets (*san-mai*, 三枚) before pushing the button with the ticket price on it. If you are going to transfer between two lines, push the button for transfers (*norikae*, 乗り換え) before pushing the price button. If at any time you make a mistake and want your money returned, push the red button to cancel (*torikeshi*, とりけし).

Not all trains on a particular line stop at all stops. Express trains (*kyūkō*, 急行) are the fastest. There are several types of express trains, including rapid, semi-, limited, and special express. Express trains are marked on the front and on the sides with the characters 急行 (*kyūkō*) written in different colors depending on the kind of express it is (red for limited express, blue for special express, and so on). If you are traveling a long distance, an express train can save a considerable amount of time. If you plan to stop at a smaller station, get off at the largest station before your stop and transfer to a local train. A local train (*kakueki teisha* or *futsū densha,* 各駅停車, 普通電車) stops at all of the stations on a line. Sometimes it waits a few minutes at a station so that the express trains can pass by. Local trains have 各駅 (*kakueki*) written in white on the fronts and the sides. The semi-express (*junkō,* 準行) stops at more stations than the express, but not as many as the local train. The semi-limited express will have 準行 (*junkō*) written in yellow or green on the front and the sides.

Buying Commuter Passes

If you travel to work or school by train, subway, or bus, you are eligible for fixed-period commuter trip passes (*teiki-ken,* 定期券). You must take the same route twice a day for more than sixteen days in a month to be eligible for a pass. Go to the window marked 定期売り場 (*teiki uriba*) or to the green window marked みどりの窓口 (*midori no madoguchi*) at the station and show your school or company ID or other proof that you work at a certain location along with the appropriate form filled out as shown on page 139.

The commuter pass allows unlimited travel between two designated stations within a designated time frame. You can purchase it on the same day you begin to use it or one day in advance. If you are renewing it, however, you can purchase it fourteen days before the expiration date. You can only use the pass between your home station and the destination station where your school or work is located. One commuter pass is good for a maximum of two railway systems (several separately owned systems serve most metropolitan areas), so if you plan to use three or more different rail systems, you may need to purchase two passes. The passes are valid for one, three, or six months and can save you a lot of money.

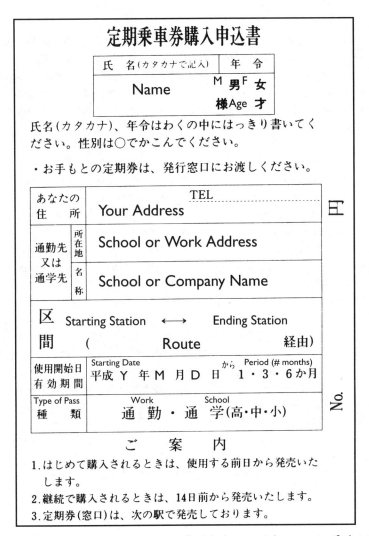

Application for a teiki-ken, or commuter pass, for ticketless transit between specified stations.

Multiple-Trip Booklets

If you only commute two or three times a week you can buy multiple-trip booklets (*kaisū-ken*, 券回数), a set of eleven tickets sold for the price of ten. Anybody can use the tickets, and one adult ticket is good for two children. They are usually valid for two to three months after the date of purchase.

Here are some travel tips for getting around Japan, both while in the city and while traveling through the countryside.

· If you need a bus, try heading toward the closest train station, which will likely be a terminus. If you need to find a taxi, head for a train station or a major hotel (although in most areas you can flag a taxi down).

· For long-distance travel, don't equate Japanese trains with Amtrak. Japanese trains are more European style—fast, on time, intelligently scheduled, and wide-ranging. Some are overnight with sleeping cars. But they are not necessarily cheap. If you will be traveling in Japan, buy a Japan Rail Pass before you enter the country so that you can move about freely.

· Be sure to get outside the main urban areas if you find yourself locked in to a job in Tokyo or Osaka. Public transportation will take you everywhere you want to go. Consider out-of-the-way destinations like Hokkaido or northern and western Honshu, or Sado Island and Okinawa (both reachable by ferries).

· To save money on food while traveling, try to stay at inexpensive Japanese inns, where the lodging usually includes a hearty breakfast (albeit Japanese style with fish, seaweed, miso broth, and rice). At lunchtime, look for lunch specials at restaurants in department stores and in areas frequented by office workers. At dinner, department stores are again a good bet, as are noodle shops. (Sushi in Japan, as in the U.S., varies widely in price.) On trains, you can usually enjoy regional cuisine from local vendors on station platforms or who board the trains with box lunches.

Orange Cards and io Cards

An Orange Card is a pass with prepaid credit and can be purchased in amounts of ¥1,000, ¥3,000, ¥5,000, and ¥10,000 at vending machines in Japan Railways (JR) stations, at ticket windows, and at Kiosk booths. When purchasing a ticket, put your Orange Card in the Orange Card vending machine and press the appropriate amount. If you have run out of credit, you can pay the difference between the ticket price and the remaining credit.

An io Card is similar to an Orange Card except that with the io Card you do not have to purchase a train ticket at a vending machine. Just put the card through the automatic ticket wicket and the amount  will be subtracted from your card until you run out of credit. Orange Cards and io Cards can also be used at fare adjustment machines.

Bullet Trains (Shinkansen)

Bullet trains (*shinkansen*, 新幹線) are ideal for travel between cities, especially cities with no airport nearby. Taking a Shinkansen can be more expensive, but it can be more convenient than taking a plane and faster than taking a bus or any other form of ground transportation. You can make reservations on a bullet train at the green window ticket counter (*midori no madoguchi*, みどりの窓口) at most Japan Railway (JR) stations, at a JR Travel Service Center (JR日本旅行センター) in major JR stations, or at travel agencies that handle Shinkansen tickets. Tickets are available up to one month prior to departure date. If you plan to travel during a busy season such as New Year's or Golden Week (the first week of May), make sure you book your reservations well in advance.

Bullet trains are quite convenient for foreigners. All of the stops are written in English, and all in-train announcements are in English. Trains are equipped with a telephone system and rest rooms, and there are vendors selling beverages and box meals. First-class "green car" tickets are available, entitling you to slightly larger seats and free magazines and beverages. If you take the Tokyo–Osaka line, note that there are two main kinds of trains, the *hikari* (ひかり), which only stops at major Shinkansen stations, and the *kodama* (こだま), which stops at every Shinkansen station. Sometimes the *nozomi* (のぞみ), which consists only of green cars and makes fewer stops, is available; although *nozomi* tickets are more expensive, it is the fastest and most comfortable way to go.

Buses

Buses comb the streets throughout Japan and are much cheaper than taxis. There are different fare systems depending on where you are. In Tokyo there is usually a flat fare. Simply board the bus and drop the fare in the box next to the driver. For some long-distance buses, the fare depends on how far you are going. There should be a sign at the bus stop where you are boarding that has the fares written next to the destination stations (although this information is usually only written in Japanese). When you board these buses, take one of the white tickets from the dispenser near the doors (you board buses through the rear doors). The ticket will have a number on it that corresponds to a fare on the electronic fare board in the front of the bus. The fare increases the farther you ride the bus; pay the fare when you get off the bus through the front doors.

It is very easy to get lost on buses in Japan. Although buses have recorded announcements for each stop and some buses have the stops electronically displayed on a screen in front of the bus, these are only in Japanese. When you hear it announced that you are getting near your stop, push the button above your seat to insure that the driver stops for you. Many Japanese streets look the same, and, unless you can read the characters for the stops, it may be hard to determine where you are. Have someone who is familiar with the local bus system go with you the first time and take notes so that the next time you can do it on your own.

Be aware that buses stop running much earlier than trains or subways. There should be a bus schedule at your stop with the departure times for all weekdays, weekends and holidays. The column for weekdays has 平日 (*heijitsu*) written above it, and the column for weekends is headed 休日 (*kyūjitsu*).

Taxis

Japan is full of taxis (*takushii*, タクシー). To catch a taxi, you can go to the taxi stands (*takushii-noriba*, タクシー乗り場) on major streets or in front of subway and train stations. You can also wave taxis down (note that in Japan traffic drives on the left). You will see a little green or red light in the lower left side of the front window. If the light is red, it means the taxi is available. If the light is green or turned off, it means that the taxi is occupied or off duty. Taxi drivers usually allow three or four passengers. When the cab driver stops to pick you up or drop you off, the rear left side door will automatically swing open. If you do not speak Japanese, have your destination written out in Japanese characters for the driver. Once you arrive at your destination pay the amount on the front meter. Tipping is not necessary, nor is it expected in Japan. If you need a receipt say, "*Ryōshūsho onegaishimasu*" and a receipt will be printed out with the fare, the cab number, and the phone number of the cab company so that you can retrieve any forgotten item. You can also purchase taxi cards (*takushii kaado*, タクシーカード) for a set amount of credit.

Buying Flight Tickets

You can purchase international flight tickets straight from the airline, but you will be paying counter price, which tends to be higher than counter prices in foreign countries. For airline phone numbers refer to the section "Important Phone Numbers and Addresses" at the back of this book. If you know the date you will travel, you may want to go through a discount travel agency known as a consolidator. These agencies buy blocks of tickets on flights at a discounted price and sell them considerably cheaper than the airlines do. Flight information can be obtained from Narita Flight Information at (0476) 34-5000 or Tokyo City Air Terminal Information at (03) 3665-7111. Airline tickets can also be purchased using any of the many Internet vendors.

You can purchase domestic airline tickets from airline counters, travel agencies, and discount ticket shops. If you buy a ticket from an airline counter you will be paying a higher price, but you may have more options available to you such as refunds or reschedules. Travel agency prices are cheaper than airline prices, but the tickets may be restricted. Many travel agencies sell tickets as part of a package, which may be a good deal if you need hotel accommodations.

Most domestic flights to and from Tokyo will depart from Haneda Airport. To get to Haneda, take the monorail direct from Hamamatsu-chō Station on the Yamanote Line in Tokyo. To get to Tokyo's international Narita Airport, see the following section.

Traveling to and from Narita Airport

N'EX

The fastest way to and from Narita Airport is the Narita Express (N'EX). It is slightly more expensive than the other options and tickets can sell out fast depending on the season. There are two types of seats available in N'EX: normal car and green car. The normal car tickets always sell out faster since they are cheaper. Green car tickets are a couple thousand yen more expensive and have little more to offer than the regular car tickets. When buying tickets at the N'EX counter at the stations ask for the regular car

> *If all you need is a plane ticket, the cheapest way may be discount ticket shops. Discount shops are usually located within sight of larger train stations. They sell airline tickets, bullet train tickets, concert tickets, movie tickets, etc. at discounted prices. If you do not speak Japanese, have someone who does go with you to the ticket shop since you will be required to confirm the reservations over the phone with the airlines. Although these tickets are cheap compared to airline counter prices, they are nonrefundable and you cannot change the date or flight once they are confirmed.*

seat. Many times the ticket vendor will sell you a green car ticket even if there are still regular seat tickets available. Sometimes it is worth it to buy a green car ticket after a long flight when all of the regular car tickets are sold out since the trains leave at one-to two-hour intervals. If you are traveling to the airport, buy your ticket in advance, especially during one of the holiday seasons. N'EX also offers standing tickets when the regular tickets are sold out. This is a nice option if you have to get to the airport and there is nothing else available. From Tokyo Station to the airport it is only fifty-three minutes, and from Shinjuku Station it is about an hour and fifteen minutes. N'EX has destination stops at Chiba, Tokyo, Shinjuku, Ikebukuro, Ōmiya, Shinagawa, Yokohama, Totsuka, and Ōfuna. Reservations are available up to one month in advance. For information on departure times call the JR East Infoline at (03) 3423-0111.

Keisei Skyliner
The Keisei Skyliner and the Keisei Limited Express (Tokkyū, 特急) are the cheapest ways to the airport. You can reserve tickets for the Skyliner at (03) 3831-0131 or through travel agencies such as Japan Travel Bureau (JTB). Reservations are not available for the Limited Express, so you must show up at the Keisei window in Ueno Station (a few stops north of Tokyo Station) thirty minutes before departure time or purchase your tickets in advance.

Limousine bus

Limousine bus service is also available. It is very cheap and sometimes just as fast as N'EX, taking seventy to ninety minutes depending on traffic conditions. This is a good alternative if you have a lot of luggage. Departures are from major hotels and from the Tokyo City Air Terminal (TCAT). Tickets are available at departure terminals or at the reservation center at (03) 3370-1156.

Automobiles

If you live in or near a major city in Japan, it is probably not practical to purchase a car. The Japanese public transportation system is one of the best in the world, and owning a car is very expensive. Tokyo traffic is bad enough already, but if everyone could afford a car the congestion would be unbearable.

Consider the following: to control congestion and encourage use of the excellent public transportation system already in place, the government has adopted various measures to discourage the use of private automobiles. For example, if you do not already possess a valid foreign license or an international license, you must obtain a Japanese license the same way a Japanese citizen does. This means taking a difficult paper test in Japanese, attending a government-approved driving school costing anywhere from ¥150,000 to ¥350,000, and then passing a road test. Second, unless you live in the countryside, you will need proof of parking. A parking spot in some places in Tokyo can cost as much as an apartment. Third, the Japanese government imposes an expensive vehicle maintenance check (*shaken*, 車 検) that must be done every two years. The price varies from car to car but is always a good percentage of the price of the car and sometimes can exceed it. Next, car insurance is compulsory. Every car owner must take out a policy of automobile third-party liability insurance or mutual relief system insurance and have the car registered. This policy also must be taken out for any motorized bicycle or moped. (It is recommended that you take out an additional policy of voluntary liability insurance.) Finally, you must pay costly gas prices—Japan is an island country with virtually no fuel resources of its own.

Unfortunately, if you live in an area where public transportation is not available, or if you have a job that requires you to drive, you may have no choice but to purchase a car.

Any foreigner at least eighteen years of age can drive in Japan if he or she has an international driver's license and a valid foreign license that is at least three months old prior to arrival in Japan. When driving in Japan, you must have both your international license and your passport with you at all times. Your license is not valid without your passport. An international license is only valid for one year after the date of issuance. If you intend to live in Japan for more than one year you might want to get a Japanese license. It is easy to get a Japanese license if you possess a valid foreign license, so be sure to keep your foreign driver's license current.

Obtaining a Japanese Driver's License

To obtain a Japanese license go to the testing site that has jurisdiction over the area where you are a registered foreigner. Bring your alien registration card, your home country license with a copy of the same, your passport, and two pictures (3 cm x 2.5 cm; these usually can be taken on the spot). You can find your test center and its phone number in the list of "Safety Driving Central Training Centers" at the back of this book. Some centers require that you have an official Japanese translation of your home country license. This can be done by the Japan Automobile Federation (JAF) for ¥2,000 to ¥3,000. You will have to take an eye examination and a test for color blindness. You will also have to take a written test in English regarding Japanese traffic laws as well as a driving test. After a few weeks, you can return to the testing center and pick up your Japanese driver's license. Renew your license about one month before the expiration date; if your license expires its renewal becomes unnecessarily complicated.

The first year you have a license is considered probationary. Japan is on a point system where each driving violation costs a certain number of points. If you exceed three points in your first licensed year, you must attend a Beginning Driver's Lecture Class (Shoshin Untensha Kyōshū, 初心運転者教習). If you do not attend you must take a re-examination. If you fail the re-examination or do not take it at all, your driver's license will be revoked.

License Renewal

A license renewal application must be submitted within a month prior to the day of expiration. If the expiration date is on a Sunday or a holiday, the renewal can be submitted on the following work day. There will be at least one window for license renewal open on Sundays in each prefecture. If you cannot make it due to overseas travel or some other legitimate reason, it is possible to make the application in advance accompanied with documents such as a passport or a doctor's certificate. You must bring your old license, one license-sized picture, and the renewal fee. When you renew your license, you must take a lecture class. You are allowed to take the simple lecture class if you had no traffic violations or accidents three years prior to renewal, or if you were eligible for the simple lecture at the previous renewal and have not had more than one minor traffic violation in the past three years. It is very important that you have your license renewed on time to avoid suspension.

Changes in Address, Name, and Other Details

Any change of name or address must be reported immediately. Present a license-sized picture with your name, and the day,

In Japan, driving under the influence of alcohol, drugs, or other stimulants carries a severe penalty; your license can be revoked on the first offense. Bear in mind that you will not be the only one held responsible if you cause an accident while under the influence: the people who drink with you, the people with you in the car, and even your guarantor or employer can be held responsible. The legal blood-alcohol content percentage is zero, so if you are going to drink at all, do not drive. If it is late and public transportation is already shut down, you can always take a taxi. Some places in Japan have a service called Unten Daikō (運転代行). If you have driven somewhere and consumed alcohol, call this service and a sober driver will drive both you and your car home for a fee.

month, and year the picture was taken. Put this information on the back of the picture (only for changes of address to a different jurisdiction) and bring a copy of your alien registration card.

Traffic Violations and Paying Fines

A traffic offender may avoid point penalties for minor offenses by paying the fine (*bakkin*, 罰金) at a post office or a bank within eight days of the offense. When a minor offense is committed, a police officer will issue a blue ticket and a notice of payment to the offender on the spot. Whether your license is suspended or revoked depends on the number of violation points accumulated during a three-year period.

There are many traffic signs in Japan that you may miss if you do not know what they mean. A partial list is on pages 151–54. The English-language book *Rules of the Road,* from the Japan Automobile Federation, describes Japan's traffic laws, regulations, and driver etiquette. It is available at any JAF center or testing center.

Japanese traffic drives on the left. Drivers from North America need to be especially cautious until they get comfortable.

Japanese Traffic and Road Signs

 Road Closed

 Closed to Large-Sized Trucks
Applies to vehicles with gross weight of 8,000 kg or more, or trucks with body length of 8 m or more.

 Closed to All Vehicles

 Closed to Large-Sized Passenger Vehicles
Applies to vehicles with fixed riding capacity of 30 passengers or more.

 No Entry for Vehicles

 Closed to Motorcycles and Motorized Bicycles

 Closed to All Vehicles Except Motorcycles

 Closed to Light Vehicles Except Bicycles

 Closed to Bicycles

 Closed to Vehicles
As shown.

 No Crossing
Vehicle crossing is prohibited (except for vehicles turning left to enter or exit a facility off the road).

 No Passing on the Right-hand Portion of the Road for Overtaking

 No U-turn

 No Overtaking

One Way Only

 One Way Only

 Designated Directions Only

 Either Direction OK

 Left Turn Only

 Either Direction OK

 No Parking or Stopping

 Motor Vehicles Only

 No Parking

 Bicycles Only

 Parking Spaces Designated

 Bicycles and Pedestrians Only

 Time-Limited Parking Zone
Parking permitted at signed locations for the period of time indicated.

 Pedestrians Only

Dangerous Goods
Prohibited
Includes gunpowder, explosives, poisons, etc.

 One Way

 Weight Limit

 Lane Distinction

 Height Limit

 Exclusive Lane for Buses

 Width Limit

 Priority Lane for Buses

 Maximum Speed Limit

 Two-Step Right Turn
for Mopeds

 Maximum Speed Limit
for Special Types of
Vehicles

 Small Right Turn for
Mopeds

 Minimum Speed Limit

Lane Driving Designations

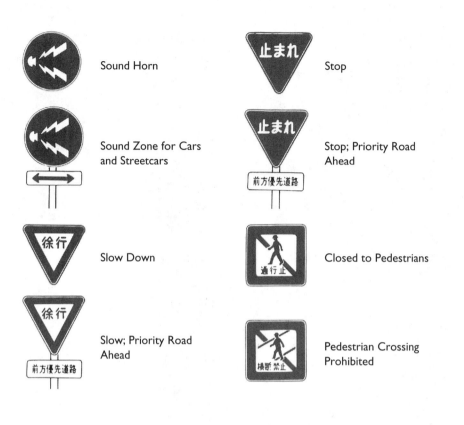

Sound Horn	Stop
Sound Zone for Cars and Streetcars	Stop; Priority Road Ahead
Slow Down	Closed to Pedestrians
Slow; Priority Road Ahead	Pedestrian Crossing Prohibited

Owning a Car

You must fulfill the following legal obligations in order to own a car in Japan:

Proof of Parking

Before purchasing a car you must prove you have a parking space, unless you live deep in the countryside where parking is not a problem. Check with others in your area to see if it is required. Some apartment buildings have parking spaces available for an extra charge. If you plan on owning a car, arrange for parking with your landlord or real estate agent.

Your parking place must be within 2 km of your residence.

You will receive the proof of parking form (*chūshajo-shōmeisho*, 駐車所証明書) from the car dealer, or, if you are purchasing a car from an individual, you can get the form from the police department. Once you have a parking place you must go to the police department in your area with the proof of parking form, a map showing where your parking space is relative to your apartment, and your name stamp (*hanko*). After you register, the police station will mail you an official registered form and a sticker that you must put in your car's back window.

Vehicle Inspection/Registration

All cars must be inspected every two years. Inspection (*shaken*, 車検) can be done at many local gas stations and repair shops. Get an estimate of how much the inspection will cost before you have it done, since different stations charge different prices for the same car. All inspected vehicles have an inspection sticker. Each year the stickers are a different color, and they indicate the year and month that the inspection expires.

Insurance

All drivers of automobiles and motorcycles are required to have automobile liability insurance to cover costs suffered by a third party who is killed or injured as a result of the operation of an automobile or any kind of motorized bicycle. Drivers in Japan must must be in possession of their insurance policy (*hoken-shōmeisho*, 保険証明書) when driving. (And you cannot obtain the mandatory vehicle inspection unless you prove you have insurance.) Make sure to report any change in the vehicle's registration number, residence, name, or any other item mentioned in the policy to the insurance company. Many drivers buy an optional policy if they feel the compulsory insurance is not enough. Four kinds of optional insurance are available: insurance for the vehicle, personal damage insurance, property damage insurance, and driver and passenger injury insurance:

- **Insurance for the vehicle**. This covers damage done to the vehicle due to collision, theft, fire, and so on. This insurance is always a contract with a deductible clause.

- **Personal damage insurance**. This provides coverage of injury to a third party not covered by liability insurance. In the case of a private passenger car, additional clauses may apply:

  a. a clause covering all the damages, irrespective of the age of the driver (basic insurance contract)

  b. a special clause excluding damage caused by a driver who is under 21 (discount of premium)

  c. a special clause excluding damage caused by a driver who is under 26 (discount of premium)

- **Property damage insurance**. This covers damage done to a third party's vehicle, building, and so on.

- **Driver and passenger injury insurance**. This covers injury of a driver or passenger while in the car, up to a fixed amount.

Accidents

If you have an accident, immediately inform your insurance company of the date of the accident, the place of the accident, the kind of damage done to the vehicle, and the number of the insurance ticket or policy. Also take photographs of the damage. Keep records of everything, including the traffic accident certificate, the report on the conditions surrounding the accident, all medical documents, and any other related papers. If you want to privately settle the dispute, the following services may be consulted free of charge:

- Prefectural Traffic Accident Consultation Offices

- Traffic Accident Consultation Offices at major city halls

- Traffic Accident Consultation Offices at local police stations

- Traffic Accident Transaction Commissions established by the local Association of Attorneys

- Traffic Consultations Bureau attached to the prefectural Traffic Safety Associations

- Traffic Accident Consultation rooms at insurance companies and their branches

- Automobile Insurance Claim Consultation Centers

- Consultation Offices of Prefectural Mutual Aid Agricultural Cooperative Associations

- Traffic Accident Dispute Settlement Centers:
  Sapporo: (011) 281-3241   Sendai: (022) 263-7231
  Tokyo: (03) 3346-1756   Nagoya: (052) 581-9491
  Osaka: (06) 6227-0277   Hiroshima: (082) 249-5421
  Takamatsu: (0878) 22-5005   Fukuoka: (092) 721-0881

Buying a Car

You could just walk into a dealership and buy a new car. But there are plenty of used cars on the market, and since most Japanese tend to take good care of their vehicles while they own them, you can probably find a decent used car at a price you can afford. Buying a car needn't be a traumatic experience. Use the information here to familiarize yourself with how cars are sold, and if need be take a friend with you to help with the business details.

Reading Advertisements for Cars

Reading an advertisement for a car is a lot like reading an advertisement for an apartment. You must know what each character or symbol in the advertisement means to know how much it will actually cost to purchase the car. Some cars may appear to be really inexpensive. Most likely the car's *shaken* is about to expire and will need to be renewed as soon as you buy it. The catalog

Ads like the one shown at right (enlarged) and below often appear in dealer windows or printed in magazines of used-car listings. The car shown at right is a red MR2 2000G with T-Bar Roof, price ¥1,180,000, 5 years old, 44,000 km on the odometer, located in Tanashi (田無).

Car Sensor has thousands of advertisements for cars of all price ranges. A typical advertisement looks like the ones shown at the bottom of page 158.

The little box on the bottom of the ad has all of the information. The price is written in boldface on the bottom left corner of the ad in units of ¥10,000. For example, the car in the example is priced at ¥1,180,000. The information inside the box varies from ad to ad, but there are some key characters you should always look for and be familiar with:

Year: 年

The year of the car will almost always be written in the Japanese system. Thus, "5 年" would refer to the fifth year of the Heisei period. Since the Heisei period started in 1989, in the Western calendar the year of the car is 1994. Refer to the "Conversions" section at the back of the book to find out how to convert Japanese years to Western years.

Mileage: 万K

The next number in the ad is usually the mileage (in kilometers) that the car has accumulated. Kilometers are represented in units of 10,000 (万), so the car in the example has 44,000 kilometers (4.4万K) on it.

Shaken Date: 検

The next number is usually the date the *shaken* is due. This is represented by the character *ken*: 検. The *shaken* of the car in this ad expires in December 1999. If *ken nashi* (検なし) is written it means there is no *shaken* and the inspection will have to be done before you can drive the car. Since the *shaken* varies from car to car, make sure you have a rough idea of the cost of the *shaken* for the particular car you are buying, regardless of whether it is about to expire or not.

At the bottom of the advertisement is a line with various symbols that are a shorthand key to the various features of the car. The key to the symbols is usually provided somewhere in the publication, but in Japanese. Here is a list of common symbols found in ads and their meanings:

❹❺❻	4, 5, 6-speed manual	⬭	CD player
4 5	4, 5, speed automatic	⊕	power steering
I	other automatics	⊞	power windows
F	fully equipped	♈	automatic locks
C	cooler	☀	sun roof
♠	air conditioner	⊛	aluminum caps
A	automatic air conditioner	⚒	had repair work
♪	cassette player	✋	never had repair work

*I*t is illegal for you or a passenger to ride a motorbike without a helmet. You must wear helmets marked with an "S" or "JIS" (Japan Industrial Standard), and the chinstrap must be firmly fastened. It is illegal to carry a passenger:
· *when the vehicle is not equipped with a passenger seat*
· *when the driver has had his license for less than a year*
· *when driving on an expressway*
Noise ordinances prohibit motorcycles with engines larger than 250 cc on some streets between 11:00 P.M. and 6:00 A.M.

Motorcycles

A motorcycle is generally cheaper than a car and a lot easier to park. It can be a very convenient commuting vehicle between home and station, school, or office. On rainy days and in ice and snow, however, you may find motorcycles inconvenient and even dangerous.

To drive a motorcycle in Japan you must have a valid license and passport as well as an international driver's license stamped for motorcycle driving. A motorcycle license for bikes up to 400 cc can be transferred. You can also get a license at any of the test centers the same way you would obtain an automobile license. You must be at least sixteen years old, get 90 of 100 questions correct on a written test, and then pass a driving test. Some people prefer motorcycles to cars since there is no requirement for a maintenance check for motorcycles up to 250 cc.

If you purchase a motorcycle, you must register it and pay a light-weight car tax. If you sell your motorcycle or move out of the ward, you must report the sale to your ward office for motorcycles up to 125 cc or to the Bureau of Traffic for motorcycles over 125 cc; otherwise you will continue to be taxed.

To register your motorcycle, you must have a certificate of sale or transfer (available at your ward office), your alien registration certificate, and your name stamp or certificate of signature.

Japan Automobile Federation (JAF)

For an enrollment fee of ¥2,000 and an annual subscription fee of ¥4,000, you can join the Japan Automobile Federation (JAF). If you break down on the road anywhere, call JAF and they will come to the rescue. As a JAF member you are entitled to:

· twenty-four-hour roadside service regardless of location or time

· free labor for the first half hour of work on the spot

· free towing for the first 5 km from the location of break-down to the garage

· touring and traveling service, insurance service, legal con-sultation service, overseas travel service, sporting service, and publication service

To join the JAF, send an application and appropriate fees to any district office. For a list of emergency rescue numbers and district offices, see the section "Important Phone Numbers and Addresses" at the back of this book.

Etiquette and Customs

Japan's rich culture has evolved over many centuries and requires a lot of experience to understand. Go to the festivals (Japan has thousands of them throughout the country every year), and take trips to local shrines and temples. Attempt to learn Japanese even if you only have the time for a few words a day. Making Japanese friends is the best way to learn about Japan. Ask questions. Japanese are very open about explaining their culture. Your whole experience in Japan is what you make of it.

This chapter is not intended to be a lesson on Japanese culture. That is for you to discover firsthand. The purpose here is to give you a general idea of proper etiquette. As a foreigner you will usually be excused for not knowing proper behavior, but it's nice to avoid being offensive if at all possible. If you are in a situation and you do not know the proper way to behave, watch the Japanese around you and follow their lead, or just ask. It is never rude to ask a question about what is proper.

Visiting Japanese Homes

In Japan, one's home is considered private. Guests are rarely invited in. But if you ever are invited to a Japanese home, there is some etiquette that should be followed.

· Bring a small gift, especially if you are staying for dinner.

Any kind of sweets, liquor, or specialty product from your home country is good.

· When entering a Japanese home, remove your shoes in the entryway of the home and put on the slippers that are provided for guests. When removing your shoes, try not to face away from host, and line your shoes up neatly with the toes facing the entryway.

· A Japanese housewife will often spend most of her time in the kitchen preparing an extravagant meal but might not actually sit down with you and the rest of the family for dinner. Do not consider this unusual.

· You will likely be offered some sort of drink or alcohol. If you are served liquor or beer, your host will fill your glass to the very brim. When the host is pouring your drink, hold your glass so that it will not spill. Then take the bottle from the host and fill his or her glass. Japanese will usually say, "*Kanpai!*" ("Cheers!") before drinking. Do not drink before the toast.

Table Manners

No one wants to be rude at the table. In order to avoid embarrassing situations, or to impress Japanese hosts with your superb table manners, here are some things you should be aware of:

· When eating at a table keep your hands above the table.

· Do not rest your elbows on the table but gently rest your arms below your wrists on the edge of the table.

· No matter how strong the temptation, do not play with your chopsticks or use them to push plates.

· Never stand your chopsticks vertically in a bowl of rice or

> **I**f you do not drink it is acceptable to ask for something nonalco-
> holic. Alcoholism in Japan is not seen the same way it is in West-
> ern countries. If you come across an uncomfortable situation where
> your host does not understand that you do not drink, you may pre-
> tend to drink or tell them that you are allergic to alcohol (which a
> number of Japanese claim to be). When you are drinking with
> friends and acquaintances in Japan and have had enough to drink,
> do not drink to the bottom of the glass. Usually the Japanese per-
> ceive an empty glass as an invitation to pour another drink.

food (this is reminiscent of the incense sticks used at Japanese funerals).

- Never pass food from your chopsticks to another's (at
  Buddhist funeral services the bones of the cremated body
  are ritually passed from one person's chopsticks to
  another's).

- Do not stab your food with chopsticks. Most Japanese
  food is prepared so that there is no need for a knife. If you
  cannot use chopsticks, ask for Western utensils. Most
  restaurants and Japanese homes have them.

- Always receive dishes or plates from the host with both
  hands unless you are at a restaurant.

- It is common to slurp when eating noodles and drinking
  tea in Japan.

- Try everything on the table no matter how unappealing it
  may look to you. Japanese think it's all right if you do not
  care for something but consider it rude if you do not at
  least try it, especially if you are at someone's house.

- Japanese say, "*Itadakimasu,*" a polite expression meaning "I
  humbly receive [this food]," when they are about to eat
  something. At the end of the meal they say, "*Gochisōsama*

deshita" ("This was a treat") to thank the host for the meal or for treating you to dinner in a restaurant.

Taking a Bath

Taking a bath in Japan is probably quite different from what you are accustomed to in your home country. Japanese do take showers, but taking a bath is considered a somewhat spiritual experience and serves more purposes than merely cleaning the body.

Always take a shower and clean yourself before getting into a Japanese bathtub. Taking a shower before taking a bath may sound silly, but the reason for this is that several people will likely be using the same bath water, which is for soaking and not washing. After you clean your body with the shower, relax in the deep Japanese bathtub. Be careful getting into the water since Japanese tend to take baths at scalding hot temperatures.

Soaking in hot water while inebriated or pregnant or if you have a heart condition is not recommended. Do not pull the plug when you are finished unless you know the bath is only intended for you.

Bathhouses

You may notice that many neighborhoods in Japan have public bathhouses (*sentō*, 銭湯). Some people use a public bathhouse if their apartments do not include bathrooms with showers. But some people go to bathhouses because they enjoy the large tubs, the atmosphere, and the hot mineral water. Some bathhouse managers do not allow foreigners in since they assume the foreigner does not know the etiquette of a Japanese bathhouse. If this happens to you, do not get upset; there are other bathhouses that will be perfectly willing to serve you. You also may not be allowed to enter if you have large tattoos. In Japan, tattoos have a

> **If you sleep on a futon, clean it and put it away properly every day.** The Japanese drape their futons over an outside railing every morning and beat it with a stick called a **futon-tataki** (布団叩) to knock out all of the dust and bed mites and to air it out. Bed mites live in the tatami, carpet, and bedding of homes. They can burrow into the skin and leave a red rash. Sunlight and heat kills the mites and their eggs. You should also regularly dust and vacuum your apartment to prevent mites from infesting your home.

negative association with gangsters, and some Japanese view tattoos as dirty.

Entrance into a bathhouse costs about ¥300. You must bring your own wash towel, soap, shampoo, and toiletries. Many bathhouses sell soap, shaving cream, and other products at inflated prices. After paying the person at the door go into either the male (男) or the female (女) changing room. Males and females bathe separately. Make sure you wash and rinse yourself off thoroughly before getting into the large bathtub. The water can be scalding hot, so always test the temperature of the bath before getting in. When you are naked and walking around the bathing area, it is polite to hold your wash towel in front of your private parts.

Sleeping

Although more and more Japanese are sleeping on Western-style beds every year, most Japanese still sleep on a futon. A Japanese futon may be quite different from the futons in your own country. The futons in the United States, for example, often resemble fold-up sofa beds. The Japanese futon has different parts, just like a Western bed. The bottom fold-up, sponge-like cushion (*matto*, マット) is laid out first (not everyone uses a *matto*). On top of this is the futon mattress called a *shikibuton* (しきぶとん). The *shiki-buton* is fitted with sheets. On top of this is a comforter blanket called a *kakebuton* (かけぶとん). The *kakebuton* has a cover that can be removed and washed. Most foreigners do not like Japanese pillows, which are smaller and much harder than Western ones. The filling of a Japanese pillow is made of little pieces of plastic straw and can take some time to become accustomed to. Softer Western pillows can be purchased but are more expensive.

Business or Name Cards

Before you leave for Japan or shortly after you arrive, have business cards (*meishi*, 名刺) made with your name and local address and phone number. Business cards are an important part of introductions in Japan. Foreigners who deal regularly with the Japanese have their names and information written in English on the front side of their cards and in Japanese on the back. Many Japanese also have their name, title, and address printed in English on the back of their business cards.

Name cards are not just used by people in business. Even Japanese high school students have name cards that they give to their friends. A name card can help facilitate introductions, especially if it is written in Japanese. If you only introduce yourself verbally, many Japanese may be hesitant to use your name out of embarrassment at attempting the difficult pronunciation. Once you have your cards made, purchase a small card holder and carry it with you at all times. You should never place cards (your own or others') in your hip pocket.

In business, cards are always given from subordinate to superior, from seller to buyer. Here are some other pointers.

· When you introduce yourself present your card face side up at chest level with both hands.

- Always receive a card with both hands and do not sit down at a meeting table or put the card away until the other person puts your card down.

- Around a conference table, you can keep cards out on the table in front of you to help you remember names; you may write the pronunciation of a person's name on their card, especially if you do not speak Japanese, but never write notes on the card or play with or fold it.

- After a talk or meeting, it is acceptable to ask someone for their card if you have not yet received one.

Weddings

A Japanese wedding reception should never be missed if you are lucky enough to be invited to one. If you get a wedding invitation, most likely it is to the reception (hirōen, 披露宴) rather than the ceremony. Most men wear black suits and white ties at weddings; women wear either kimono or formal dresses. Instead of wedding presents, Japanese give money (oshūgi, お祝儀) in a special wedding envelope (shūgibukuro, 祝儀袋), usually ¥30,000 in fresh, crisp bills. (Never give ¥40,000, since the word for "four," shi, also means "death" and is considered unlucky). In return you receive various presents from the new bride and groom, such as teacups, Japanese sweets, and almost always a smoked whitefish (a pun on the word tai, which means "whitefish" and is also a syllable in the Japanese word for "Congratulations": Omedetai).

Funerals

Most Japanese funerals are conducted in the Buddhist tradition. A wake is held the night before for friends and acquaintances to pay their last respects. If there is a reception desk, offer your condolence money (*kōden*, 香奠) in the proper envelope (*noshibukuro*, のしぶくろ) or place it in the enamel tray next to the register and sign in. Just before you reach the altar, bow to the family and priest and then bow to the picture of the deceased. Take a pinch of incense from the bowl on the altar with your thumb, index, and middle finger and raise it to eye level before sprinkling it onto the burner. Watch other Japanese to see what they do and follow their lead. Men should wear a black suit and a black tie; women should wear a black dress or suit.

Gift Giving

Whether it is a free gift from Mister Donut or a souvenir from a friend returning from a day trip, Japanese love to exchange presents. It is very easy to get caught up in an endless cycle of gift giving in Japan, reciprocating gifts with more gifts. Following Japanese customs and traditions will always be appreciated, but in general, foreigners are excused for not knowing the cultural guidelines for gift giving. Japanese will always be pleased if you show you are putting some effort into learning their customs and grateful when you manage to follow the seasonal gift-giving guidelines correctly.

Below is a list of the typical gift-giving seasons and the appropriate etiquette for each occasion:

New Year's: January 1–3

Send New Year's postcards to friends and associates. Make sure to mail them by mid-December in order for them to be received by January 1. Return postcards can be mailed to those you may have forgotten to send a card to but from whom you received a card. On New Year's children receive what is called *otoshidama* money from relatives.

Oseibo

Oseibo (お歳暮) is for year-end gift exchanges, generally from inferiors to superiors but also to anyone who has shown you kindness during the year. Something edible should be given, such as Japanese sweets or liquor in the ¥3,000–5,000 range. Return a thank-you card and a gift half a year later at *ochūgen*.

Ochūgen: July 1–13

Ochūgen (お中元) is the midsummer gift exchange from superiors to subordinates. Give the same kind of gift as described above for *oseibo*. Return a thank-you card.

Birthday

As in most countries, birthday presents are given to friends and acquaintances. Whatever you think is appropriate will suffice. It is the thought that counts. Return a thank-you card.

Wedding

Gift money is handed to the receptionist at the wedding, usually ¥30,000. Guests receive a bag of gifts in return.

Wedding Anniversary

Special gifts are given on the 1st, 7th, 15th, 25th, and 30th anniversaries. No return gift is expected.

New Baby

Clothes, toys, and sometimes cash are given to the parents of a newly born healthy baby within one to two weeks of the birth. A small wooden bowl or a cup with the baby's name is given in return. A thank-you card is also acceptable.

Hospital Visit

Give flowers (no potted plants because this implies a long stay), books, etc. Return a thank-you card

Funeral

Give at least ¥5,000 to the family of the deceased to help pay for funeral expenses and all the gifts you will receive in return.

Admission to School

Give school-related items following a child's entrance into elementary school. *Sekihan* (a Japanese rice and bean sweet) or a thank-you card is given in response.

Omiyage: Souvenirs

The most common gift in Japan is *omiyage* (おみやげ), souvenir gifts you bring back from trips for friends, coworkers, and other acquaintances. *Omiyage* are sold everywhere in Japan, from the busiest areas in Tokyo to the most remote parts of the country. A good *omiyage* is usually some kind of food, tea, or snack that the recipient can share with his or her family or other coworkers. Even if you go on only a brief weekend trip, always remember to bring back a small treat for your coworkers, landlord, or friends.

Japanese Holidays and Special Days

Japanese holidays are evenly spaced throughout the year, except for a cluster at New Year's and at Golden Week in springtime. National holidays in the listings below are indicated by an asterisk (*). If a holiday falls on a Sunday, it is generally observed the following Monday.

* New Year's Day (Ganjitsu, 元日): January 1
New Year's Holiday (O-Shōgatsu, お正月): January 1–3

New Year's Day is Japan's biggest holiday, equivalent to Christmas in Western nations. Japanese send New Year's postcards (*nengajō*, 年賀状) that can be purchased or handmade to give thanks to acquaintances and relatives for favors received and to wish them health and happiness throughout the coming year. It is customary to greet everyone you see for the first time in the new year with, "*Akemashite omedetō gozaimasu.*" You can also say, "*Kotoshi mo yoroshiku onegaishimasu,*" which means you hope you will continue on good terms throughout the coming year. The 1st through the 3rd of January are national holidays. During this period Japanese go on visits (*nenshimawari*, 年始回り) to their closer friends' and relatives' houses. Adults give children a New Year's gift of money (*otoshidama*, お年玉). Sometime during the holiday Japanese will visit the local shrine to make their New Year's wishes. New Year's is one of the busiest traveling seasons in Japan. Buy reserved seat tickets well in advance and allow plenty of time to get through the crowded stations.

* Coming of Age Day (Seijin no Hi, 成人の日): 2nd Monday in January

Coming of Age Day is for young people who have turned or will turn twenty, the age considered the beginning of adulthood. The new adults dress up in kimono or suits and visit local shrines for special ceremonies.

Setsubun (節分): February 3 or 4

Setsubun is an old tradition adopted from China. It marks the end of winter according to the lunar calendar. Japanese symbolically sweep out bad spirits and misfortune and invite in luck, scattering soybeans while chanting, *"Fuku wa ie, oni wa soto"* ("In with fortune, out with the devils").

* National Foundation Day (Kenkoku Kinenbi, 建国記念日): February 11

National Foundation Day celebrates the day the first Japanese emperor, Jinmu, ascended to the throne over 2,600 years ago.

Valentine's Day: February 14

On Valentine's Day in Japan, women give men chocolates. Women get their turn to receive candy in March on White Day.

Doll Festival (Hina Matsuri, ひな祭): March 3

The Doll Festival is another tradition that originated in China and is celebrated to wish for a daughter's healthy growth. Paper dolls are displayed to remove any impurities from the daughter and are then put into a stream where they float away.

White Day: March 14

This is the reciprocal of Valentine's Day. On White Day, men give women chocolate (usually white chocolate).

Spring Equinox (Ohigan, お彼岸): latter half of March

The one week near the vernal or the spring equinox is when Japanese clean the household Buddhist altar and decorate it with flowers and rice cakes (*botamochi*, ぼたもち) as offerings to their ancestors.

* Vernal Equinox Day (Shunbun no Hi, 春分の日): between March 19 and 21

This national holiday celebrates the first day of spring.

* Greenery Day (Midori no Hi, みどりの日): April 29

Greenery Day celebrates the birthday of the Shōwa Emperor, who died in 1989. It is called Green Day in honor of his appreciation of nature. It is the first of the Golden Week holidays, a cluster of national holidays that many Japanese use as an opportunity to travel or relax. Schools are on vacation and most companies are closed during this period. If you plan to travel during Golden Week, buy reserved seat tickets well in advance and allow plenty of extra time to make your connections.

* Constitution Memorial Day (Kenpō Kinenbi, 憲法記念日): May 3

The anniversary of the adoption of the national constitution in 1947 is the second day of Golden Week.

* People's Day (Kokumin no Kyūjitsu, 国民の休日): May 4

People's Day has no special meaning, but it fits nicely into Golden Week to provide the Japanese a five-day vacation.

* Children's Day (Kodomo no Hi, 子供の日): May 5

Children's Day is the final day of Golden Week. In ancient times, Japanese samurai warriors would hang their armor out to dry. Now on this day, warrior dolls (*musha ningyō*, 武者人形) are displayed with a *shobu* iris plant to ward off evil. A carp streamer (*koinobori*, 鯉のぼり) is flown as a prayer for the healthy growth of children.

Mother's Day (Haha no Hi, 母の日): 2nd Sunday of May

Mother's Day in Japan is similar to that celebrated in the U.S.

Father's Day (Chichi no Hi, 父の日): 3rd Sunday of June

Father's Day in Japan is similar to to that celebrated in the U.S.

Star Festival (Tanabata Matsuri, 七夕祭): July 7

The Star Festival recalls an old Chinese fable of forbidden love between a princess and a farm boy. According to the fable, the lovers were turned into stars that only cross paths one night a year, represented by the stars Vega and Altair, whose paths cross each other on this night. Japanese celebrate this romantic day by hanging large banners and streamers decorated with love poems.

* Maritime Day (Umi no Hi, 海の日): July 20

This new holiday was provided by the government to give the general population a much-needed day off in the summer and to show appreciation to the ocean. Japan, after all, is an island nation.

O-Bon (お盆): mid-July or mid-August

During O-Bon, deceased ancestors' spirits are said to return to the home. To greet them, Japanese decorate and place offerings at the household Buddhist altar. O-Bon is when many Japanese who work in the cities return to their hometowns. Trains are crowded, so if you are going to travel during this time, make sure you buy reserved seat tickets well in advance.

* Respect for the Aged Day (Keirō no Hi, 敬老の日): September 15

Respect for the Aged Day celebrates the long lives of the elderly.

* Autumnal Equinox Day (Shūbun no Hi, 秋分の日): between September 21 and 25

The first day of autumn is a time to remember one's ancestors.

* Health-Sports Day (Tai-iku no Hi, 体育の日): October 10.

Health-Sports Day commemorates the Tokyo Olympics, a memorable event in Japan's postwar history, and encourages citizens to participate in sports and lead healthy lives.

* Culture Day (Bunka no Hi, 文化の日): November 3

Culture Day is one of Japan's oldest holidays and commemorates the birth of the Meiji Emperor in 1852. Artists and performers are honored on this day.

Shichi-Go-San (七五三): November 15

Shichi-Go-San, meaning "seven-five-three," is when children of these ages are dressed in traditional clothes and taken to local shrines to pray for good luck.

* Labor Thanksgiving Day (Kinrō Kansha no Hi, 勤労感謝の日): November 23

Labor Thanksgiving Day honors working people.

* Emperor's Birthday (Tennō Tanjōbi, 天皇誕生日): December 23

December 23 is Emperor Akihito's birthday. This is the only day of the year the imperial palace is open to the public.

Christmas: December 25

Christmas in Japan is an interesting experience for Westerners. Japanese, unless they are Christian, do not celebrate the religious aspect of the holiday. Rather, Christmas is when young couples go on romantic dates. Restaurant prices are considerably higher, and expensive "Christmas cakes" are sold for sharing with the family.

Ō-Misoka (大みそか): December 31

On the last day of the year, Japanese clean their houses from top to bottom and attach a pine branch and rope ornament (*shime-kazari*, しめ飾り) to the home. Special New Year's foods called *osechi ryōri* (お節料理) are prepared in advance and eaten over the course of the New Year's holiday. On the evening of December 31, Japanese eat soba noodles that symbolize long life and visit their local shrine to make wishes for the coming year.

Conversions

Length

1 inch = 2.54 cm

1 foot = 0.305 m

1 yard = 0.914 m

1 mile = 1.609 km

1 cm = 0.394 in

1 m = 39.37 in = 1.09 yd

1 km = 0.621 mi

Weight

1 oz = 28.35 g

1 lb = 16 oz = 453.6 g

14 lb = 1 stone

1 g = 0.035 oz

1 kg = 2.2 lb

1 stone = 6.35 kg

Volume

1 UK gal = 4.54 liters

1 US gal = 3.78 liters

1 UK fl oz = 28.41 ml

1 US fl oz = 1.041 UK fl oz = 29.6 ml

1 liter = 0.22 UK gal

1 liter = 0.265 US gal

Temperature

$$F° = (C° \times 9/5) + 32° \qquad C° = (F° \times 5/9) - 32°$$

Normal body temperature: 98.6° F = 37° C

Weather

-10° C = 14° F   25° C = 77° F

  0° C = 32° F   30° C = 86° F

10° C = 50° F   35° C =95° F

20° C = 68° F   40° C =104° F

Approximations of common oven temperatures

140° F = 60° C   400° F = 205° C

275° F = 135° C   425° F = 220° C

325° F = 165° C   450° F = 230° C

350° F = 175° C   475° F = 245° C

375° F = 190° C   500° F = 260° C

Cooking

1 T = 14.79 ml   1 cup = 236.6 ml = 16 T

1 liter = 1.06 qt

1 pt = 2 cups = 16 fl oz = $^1/_2$ qt = $^1/_8$ gal

Clothing Sizes

Men

Jacket

JAPAN	A4	A5	A6	A7	AB4	AB5	AB6	AB7
USA/UK	36ES	37S	38S	39R	38ES	39S	40S	41R
EUROPE	44-6	46-6	48-6	50-6	44-4	46-4	48-4	50-4

Shirts

JAPAN	36	37	38	39	40	41	42
USA/UK	14	14^1/$_2$	15	15^1/$_2$	16	16^1/$_2$	17
EUROPE	35	37	38	39	40	41	42

Jackets, sweaters, underwear, sports shirts, etc.

Designation	S	M	L	LL	EL
Chest Circumference	78–86 cm	84–92 cm	90–98 cm	96–104	102–110 cm
Height		150–160 cm	160–170 cm	170–180 cm	175–185 cm	175–185 cm
Waist Circumference	66–74 cm	72–88 cm	78–88 cm	86–96 cm	94–104 cm

Body types

Body Size	Y	YA	A	AB	B	BE	E
Drop Size	16	14	12	10	8	4	0

Example: A 38–78 cm = Body type A, Neck 38, Sleeve 78

Shoes

JAPAN	24	24.5	25	25.5	26	26.5	27	27.5
USA/UK	6	6^1/$_2$	7–7^1/$_2$	8	8^1/$_2$	9–9^1/$_2$	10–10^1/$_2$	11
EUROPE	38	39	40	41	42	43	44	45

Women

Dresses, blouses

JAPAN	9	11	13	15						
USA	10	12	14	16	18	20	40	42	44	46
FRANCE	38	40	42	44	46	48	50	52	54	56
UK	32	34	36	38	40	42				

Shoes

JAPAN	22.5	23	23.5	24	24.5	25	25.5	26
USA/UK	$4-4^1/_2$	$5-5^1/_2$	6	$6^1/_2$	$7-7^1/_2$	$8^1/_2$	9	$9^1/_2-10$
EUROPE	34	35	36	37	38	39	40	41

Stockings

JAPAN	$20^1/_4$	$21^1/_4$	$22^3/_4$	24	$25^1/_4$	$26^1/_2$
USA/UK	8	$8^1/_2$	9	$9^1/_2$	10	$10^1/_2$
EUROPE	$20^1/_4$	$21^1/_2$	$23^3/_4$	24	$25^1/_4$	$26^1/_2$

Body types

Type A: Ordinary proportions (bust, hip, height, etc.)

Type Y: Same as A except somewhat smaller hip

Type AB: Same as A but somewhat larger hip and waist

Type B: Somewhat larger overall than AB

Height code

Height cm	145	150	155	160	165	170	175	180	185
Code		0	1	2	3	4	5	6	7	8

Bust code

Bust cm	73	76	79	82	85	88	91	94	97	100
Code	3	5	7	9	11	13	15	17	19	21

Example: 9A2 = Bust 82, Ordinary Proportions, Height 155

Down jackets, parkas, coats, etc.

Size	S	M	L	LL	EL
Chest Circumference	72–80	79–87	86–94	93–101	100–108
Height		145–155	150–160	155–165	160–170	160–170

Calendar Years

The Japanese use two different kinds of dating systems to indicate the year. The Western calendar is used for everyday purposes—but the Japanese calendar is used for important dates in history, birth dates, and major events. In the Japanese calendar, each period of an emperor's reign begins at year 1. Thus, when Emperor Hirohito died in 1989, that year, which had been year 64 of the Shōwa era, became year 1 of the current Heisei era. It is a good idea to memorize your own birth date in the Japanese system since it will be required on many documents. To calculate your birth date using the Japanese calendar (assuming you were not born in the Heisei era), subtract the last year of the era before the era your birth year falls in from your birth year. Following are the beginning years of the periods since the Meiji period:

Meiji (明治) 1868   Taishō (大正) 1912

Shōwa (昭和) 1926   Heisei (平成) 1989

Example 1: If you were born in 1981, your birth year in the Japanese calendar is 1981 minus 1925 = Shōwa 56.

(Subtract 1925 since 1981 is in the Shōwa period and 1925 is the last year before the Shōwa period began.)

Example 2: If you were born in 1966, your Japanese birth year is Shōwa 41 (1966–1925 = 41) .

Important Phone Numbers and Addresses

Emergency Phone Numbers

Police	110
Fire and Ambulance	119
Hospital Information (Tokyo)	(03) 3212-2323

Embassies and Consulates

Embassies

Australia	(03) 5232-4111
Austria	(03) 3451-8281
Belgium	(03) 3262-0191
Brazil	(03) 3404-5211
Canada	(03) 3408-2101
China	(03) 3452-7561
Ethiopia	(03) 3718-1003
France	(03) 5420-8800
Germany	(03) 3473-0151
Greece	(03) 3403-0871
India	(03) 3262-2391

Indonesia	(03) 3441-4201
Iran	(03) 3446-8011
Ireland	(03) 3263-0695
Israel	(03) 3264-0911
Italy	(03) 3453-5291
Jamaica	(03) 5721-4114
Kenya	(03) 3723-4006
Korea	(03) 3452-7611
Malaysia	(03) 3476-3840
Mexico	(03) 3581-1131
New Zealand	(03) 3467-2271
Philippines	(03) 3496-2731
Russia	(03) 3583-4224
Saudi Arabia	(03) 3589-5241
Singapore	(03) 3586-9111
South Africa	(03) 3265-3366
Spain	(03) 3583-8531
Sri Lanka	(03) 3585-7431
Sweden	(03) 5562-5050
Switzerland	(03) 3473-0121
Thailand	(03) 3441-7352
United Kingdom	(03) 3265-5511
United States	(03) 3224-5000
Vietnam	(03) 3466-3311

Consulate General Offices

Australia

Sapporo Consulate	(011) 242-4381
Sendai Consulate	(022) 265-6810
Nagoya Consulate	(052) 211-0630
Osaka Consulate	(06) 6941-9271
Fukuoka Consulate	(092) 734-5055

Canada
Nagoya Consulate   (052) 972-0450
Osaka Consulate   (06) 6212-4910
Fukuoka Consulate   (092) 752-6055

United Kingdom
Osaka Consulate   (06) 6281-1616

United States
Sapporo Consulate   (011) 641-1115
Osaka Consulate   (06) 6315-5900
Fukuoka Consulate   (092) 751-9331
Naha Consulate   (098) 876-4211
Nagoya Consulate   (052) 203-4011

Immigration Offices

Regional Immigration Bureaus and District Immigration Offices

Tokyo Regional Immigration Bureau
1-3-1 Ōtemachi, Chiyoda-ku, Tokyo 100-0004
(03) 3286-5241
Tokyo, Kanagawa, Saitama, Chiba, Ibaraki, Tochigi, Gunma, Yamanashi, Nagano, Niigata

Yokohama District Immigration Office
37-9 Yamashita-chō, Naka-ku, Yokohama-shi, Kanagawa 231-0023
(045) 661-5110
Kanagawa

Narita Airport District Immigration Office
1-1 Furugome, Narita-shi, Chiba 282-0004

(0476) 34-2221
Narita Airport

Osaka Regional Immigration Bureau
2-1-17 Tani-machi, Chūō-ku, Osaka 540-0012
(06) 6941-0771
Osaka, Kyoto, Hyōgo, Nara, Shiga, Wakayama

Kansai Airport District Immigration Office
Senshū-kūkō, Tajiri-chō, Osaka 549-0011
(0724) 55-1453
Kansai Airport

Kobe District Immigration Office
Kaigan-dōri, Chūō-ku, Kobe-shi, Hyōgo 650-0024
(078) 391-6377
Hyōgo

Nagoya Regional Immigration Bureau
4-3-1 Sannomaru, Naka-ku, Nagoya-shi, Aichi 460-0001
(052) 951-2391
Aichi, Mie, Gifu Shizuoka, Fukui, Toyama, Ishikawa

Hiroshima Regional Immigration Bureau
6-30 Kami-hatchōbori, Naka-ku, Hiroshima-shi, Hiroshima 730-0012
(082) 221-4411
Hiroshima, Okayama, Yamaguchi, Tottori, Shimane

Fukuoka Regional Immigration Bureau
1-22 Okihama-machi, Hakata-ku, Fukuoka-shi, Fukuoka 812-0031
(092) 281-7431
Fukuoka, Saga, Ōita, Nagasaki, Kumamoto, Kagoshima, Miyazaki, Okinawa

Naha District Immigration Office
1-15-15 Higawa, Naha-shi, Okinawa 900-0022

(098) 832-4185
Okinawa

Sendai Regional Immigration Bureau
1-23-20 Gorin, Miyagino-ku, Sendai-shi, Miyagi 983-0842
(022) 256-6076
Miyagi, Fukushima, Yamagata, Iwate, Akita, Aomori

Sapporo Regional Immigration Bureau
12 Odori-Nishi, Chūō-ku, Sapporo-shi, Hokkaido 060-0042
(011) 261-7502
Hokkaido

Takamatsu Regional Immigration Bureau
1-1 Marunouchi, Takamatsu-shi, Kagawa 760-0033
(0878) 22-5852
Kagawa, Ehime, Tokushima, Kōchi

Immigration Centers

Ōmura Immigration Center
595-2 Kogashima-machi, Ōmura-shi, Nagasaki 856-0817
(0957) 52-2121

Higashi-Nihon Immigration Center
1766 Hisano-chō, Ushiku-shi, Ibaraki 300-1200
(0298) 75-1291

Nishi-Nihon Immigration Center
1-11-1 Kōriyama, Ibaraki-shi, Osaka 567-0071
(0726) 41-8152

Information Phone Numbers

General Information

NTT Information in English
Tokyo	(03) 5295-1010
Narita	(0476) 28-1010
Yokohama	(045) 322-1010
Osaka	(06) 6313-1010
Nagoya	(052) 541-1010
Hiroshima	(082) 262-1010
Sapporo	(011) 219-1010
Sendai	(022) 232-1010
Fukuoka	(092) 632-1010
NTT Information (Japanese)	104
Time	117
Weather	177
Kimi Information Center	(03) 3986-1604

Postal Information

Postal Mailing Service Information	(03) 5472-5851
Individual Postal Banking Information	(048) 600-3570

Daily Living Information

Japan Hotline	(03) 3586-0110
Yoke Community Lounge Information Corner	(045) 671-7209

Tourist Information

Asakusa Tourist Information Center	(03) 3842-5566
Atami City Tourist Information Association—Izu	(0557) 85-2222
Fuji Visitor's Center	(0555) 72-0259
Ito Tourist Association	(0555) 37-6105
JNTO Tourist Information Centers	
Tokyo	(03) 3201-3331
Kyoto	(075) 371-5649
Japan Railways East Information	(03) 3423-0111
Japan Travel Phone (Toll Free)	
Eastern Japan	(0120) 222-800
Western Japan	(0120) 444-800
Kanagawa Prefectural Tourist Association	(045) 681-0007
Shimoda City Tourist Association	(0558) 22-1531
Teletourist	(03) 3503-2911

English-Language Newspapers

The Daily Yomiuri	(0120) 43-1159
Mainichi Daily News	(03) 3212-0885
International Herald Tribune / Asahi Shimbun	(0120) 45-6371
The Japan Times	(0120) 03-6242

Transportation Phone Numbers

Airport Flight Information	
Haneda Airport	(03) 5757-8111
Narita Airport	(0476) 34-5000

(0476) 32-2800

Tokyo City Air Terminal (TCAT)	(03) 3423-0111
JR East Infoline	(03) 3423-0111
Subway Information Service	(03) 3837-7111
Lost and Found	
Eidan (Teito) Subways	(03) 3834-5577
JR	(03) 3231-1880
Taxi	(03) 3648-0300
Toei Bus/Subway	(03) 3818-5760
Keisei Skyliner Information	(03) 3831-0131
Airport Limousine Bus Information	(03) 3665-7220

Airlines

(Most ticket agents can speak English.)

Air China	(03) 3505-2021
Air France	(03) 3475-1511
Air India	(03) 3214-1981
Air New Zealand	(03) 3287-1641
Air Pacific	(03) 3593-7030
Alitalia	(03) 3580-2181
All Nippon Airways	(03) 3592-3468
American Airlines	(03) 3248-2011
America West Airlines	(03) 5251-2761
Asiana Airlines	(03) 5472-6600
Austrian Airlines	(03) 3582-2231
British Airways	(03) 3593-8811
Canadian Airlines International	(03) 3281-7426
China Airlines	(03) 3436-1661
China Eastern Airlines	(03) 3505-2021
Continental Airlines	(03) 3592-1631
Delta Airlines	(03) 5275-7000
Egypt Air	(03) 3211-4521
Finnair	(03) 3222-6801

Hong Kong Dragon Airlines	(03) 3589-5315
Iran Air	(03) 3586-2101
Japan Airlines	(03) 5489-1111
Japan Air System	(03) 3438-1155
Japan Asia Airways	(03) 3455-7511
KLM Royal Dutch Airlines	(03) 3216-0771
Korean Air	(03) 3211-3311
Lufthansa Airlines	(03) 3580-2111
Malaysia Airlines	(03) 3503-5961
Northwest Airlines	(03) 3533-6000
Olympic Airways	(03) 3583-1911
Pakistan International Airlines	(03) 3216-6511
Philippine Airlines	(03) 3593-2421
Qantas Airways	(03) 3593-7000
Scandinavian Airlines	(03) 3503-8101
Singapore Airlines	(03) 3213-3431
Swiss Air	(03) 3212-1016
Thai Airways International	(03) 3503-3311
Turkish Airlines	(03) 3595-2901
United Airlines	(03) 3817-4411
UTA French Airlines	(03) 3475-1511
Virgin Atlantic Airlines	(03) 5269-2680

Road Conditions

Akita	(0188) 62-7744
Aomori	(0177) 77-5555
Chiba	(043) 243-2311
Chūbu	(052) 954-8888
Chūbu Expressway	(0586) 77-3179
Chūgoku	(082) 221-7777
Chūgoku Expressway	(082) 877-9292
Ehime	(089) 933-2331
Fukui	(0776) 26-1010

Gifu	(058) 272-3611
Gunma	(0272) 23-7474
Hokkaido	(011) 281-6511
Hokuriku Expressway	(0762) 49-1852
Hyōgo	(078) 371-1141
Ibaraki	(029) 226-2531
Ishikawa	(0762) 63-4541
Iwate	(0196) 24-2100
Kagoshima	(099) 226-8400
Kanagawa	(045) 212-1111
Kanetsu Chūō Expressway	(0426) 91-0058
Kansai	(06) 6313-1141
Kinki Expressway	(06) 6877-1830
Kita Kyushu	(093) 582-1331
Kōchi	(0888) 66-1121
Kumamoto	(096) 382-8686
Kyoto	(075) 431-1141
Kyushu	(092) 651-1331
Kyushu Expressway	(092) 925-4000
Mie	(0592) 26-7151
Miyazaki	(0985) 25-5000
Nagano	(026) 244-0011
Nagasaki	(0958) 21-1331
Nationwide, Kantō	(03) 3264-1331
Niigata	(025) 283-5252
Ōita	(0975) 32-8888
Okayama	(0862) 54-6111
Okinawa	(098) 866-4840
Saga	(0952) 22-7711
Saitama	(048) 833-1133
Shiga	(0775) 22-1141
Shikoku	(0878) 34-3400
Shikoku Expressway	(0878) 23-8188
Shimane	(0852) 21-3000

Shizuoka	(054) 252-1111
Shuto Expressway	(03) 3239-9801
Tochigi	(028) 621-1100
Tōhoku	(022) 225-7711
Tōhoku Expressway	(0196) 38-8770
Tōhoku Jōban Expressway	(048) 757-2039
Tokushima	(0886) 22-3344
Tokyo Expressways (recorded)	(03) 3264-0222
Tokyo Main Roads (recorded)	(03)3581-0333
Tokyo Metropolis	(03) 3581-7611
Tokyo Metropolis (recorded)	(03) 3236-0111
Tokyo Shuto Expressways (recorded)	(03) 3221-0555
Tōmei Expressway	(044) 866-3410
Tottori	(0857) 28-3700
Toyama	(0764) 32-2223
Yamagata	(0236) 31-3335
Yamaguchi	(0839) 22-6622
Yamanashi	(0552) 32-5000

Safety Driving Central Training Centers

Aichi	(052) 954-8930
Akita	(0188) 63-8811
Aomori	(0177) 82-5074
Chiba	(043) 276-3040
Ehime	(089) 978-1999
Fukui	(0776) 51-3980
Fukuoka	(092) 641-6364
Fukushima	(0245) 91-4111
Gifu	(058) 274-1000
Gunma	(0272) 53-1102
Hakodate	(0138) 55-7500
Hiroshima	(082) 227-4011
Hyōgo	(078) 304-0205

Ibaraki	(029) 293-8822
Ishikawa	(0762) 37-5900
Iwate	(0196) 53-1871
Kagawa	(0878) 82-3399
Kagoshima	(099) 269-7575
Kanagawa	(045) 364-7000
Kōchi	(0888) 92-5221
Kumamoto	(096) 383-5566
Kyoto	(075) 631-7600
Mie	(0592) 34-5165
Miyagi	(022) 373-7171
Miyazaki	(0985) 29-3456
Nagano	(026) 292-5111
Nagasaki	(0958) 25-4591
Nara	(07442) 3-7171
Niigata	(025) 256-2344
Ōita	(0975) 49-3161
Okayama	(0867) 24-4360
Okinawa	(098) 868-7571
Osaka	(06) 6909-5821
Saga	(0952) 29-0335
Saitama	(0485) 41-2411
Shiga	(0775) 85-3456
Shimane	(0852) 36-6255
Shizuoka	(054) 252-3191
Tochigi	(0289) 76-1411
Tokushima	(0886) 63-1101
Tokyo	(0423) 65-3211
Tottori	(0857) 28-6221
Toyama	(0764) 51-1840
Wakayama	(0734) 72-4433
Yamagata	(0236) 55-3456
Yamaguchi	(0839) 24-4151
Yamanashi	(0552) 85-2345

Traffic Safety Associations

Information about renewing a driver's license, lecture classes on driving skills, traffic accident consultation, and material to assist in road traffic safety are all available at the following offices.

Aichi	(052) 981-7587	(052) 981-7588
Akita	(0188) 36-2505	(0188) 36-6754
Aomori	(0177) 82-5012	
Chiba	(043) 271-8481	
Ehime	(089) 979-2101	
Fukui	(0776) 22-0465	
Fukuoka	(092) 641-8880	
Fukushima	(0245) 91-5038	(0245) 91-3688
Gifu	(058) 271-5278	(058) 263-9337
Gunma	(0272) 52-0251	(0272) 53-9080
Hiroshima	(082) 227-2161	(082) 227-0220
Hokkaido	(011) 241-1725	(011) 232-2851
Hyōgo	(078) 341-8318	(078) 371-2262
Ibaraki	(029) 247-3355	(029) 247-3356
Ishikawa	(0762) 38-0496	
Iwate	(0196) 52-4597	
Kagawa	(0878) 34-4556	
Kagoshima	(099) 269-7565	(099) 224-3598
Kanagawa	(045) 481-0766	(045) 481-0767
Kōchi	(0888) 22-5877	
Kumamoto	(096) 384-0682	(096) 385-2383
Kyoto	(075) 231-9151	(075) 451-3343
Mie	(0592) 28-9636	(0592) 23-1333
Miyagi	(022) 223-1130	
Miyazaki	(0985) 51-4078	
Nagano	(026) 292-9750	
Nagasaki	(0958) 24-7331	(0958) 25-8687
Nara	(07442) 2-0680	
Niigata	(025) 285-3755	(025) 285-3756

Ōita	(0975) 32-0815	
Okayama	(0862) 24-3003	
Okinawa	(098) 868-2860	(098) 863-7456
Osaka	(06) 6941-6983	(06) 6443-6520
Saga	(0952) 26-9837	
Saitama	(048) 824-3050	(048) 541-5588
Shiga	(0775) 85-2750	(0775) 25-9180
Shimane	(0852) 36-6337	
Shizuoka	(054) 251-4765	
Tochigi	(028) 622-8483	(028) 645-4405
Tokushima	(0886) 24-2525	
Tokyo	(03) 3592-1234	(03) 3248-1330
Tottori	(0857) 24-2110	
Toyama	(0764) 51-1851	(0764) 51-1852
Wakayama	(0734) 73-1710	
Yamagata	(0236) 55-5320	(0236) 22-3299
Yamaguchi	(08397) 3-0054	
Yamanashi	(0552) 37-7827	

Japan Automobile Federation (JAF)

District Offices

Hokkaido District Office
1-1-1 Fukuzumi-sanjō, Toyohira-ku, Sapporo-shi 062-0043
Tel (011) 857-712

Kantō District Office
3-11-6 Ōtsuka, Bunkyō-ku, Tokyo 112-8638
(03) 5976-9285

Kansai District Office
1-13-3 Shin-machi, Nishi-ku, Osaka 550-0013
(06) 6543-5841

Shikoku District Office
591 Matsunawa-chō, Takamatsu-shi, Kagawa 760-0079
(0878) 67-8411

Tōhoku District Office
3-8-105 Oroshimachi, Wakabayashi-ku, Sendai-shi, Miyagi 984-0015
(022) 783-2850

Chūbu District Office
3-7-56 Fukue, Shōwa-ku, Nagoya-shi, Aichi 466-0059
(052) 872-1163

Chūgoku District Office
2-9-3 Kogo-kita, Nishi-ku, Hiroshima-shi, Hiroshima 733-8610
(082) 272-0321

Kyushu District Office
5-12-27 Muromi, Sawara-ku, Fukuoka-shi, Fukuoka 814-8505
(092) 841-7731

JAF Offices to Call in Case of a Breakdown

Aichi	(052) 833-53000
Akita	(0188) 66-0111
Aomori	(0177) 44-0110
Asahikawa	(0166) 53-8828
Chiba	(043) 224-1655
Ehime	(089) 958-0111
Fukui	(0776) 25-2560
Fukuoka	(092) 841-5000
Fukushima	(0245) 46-0110
Gifu	(058) 246-9555
Gunma	(0273) 63-5141
Hakodate	(0138) 49-5654
Hiroshima	(082) 272-4949

Hyōgo	(078) 303-0111
Ibaraki	(029) 244-0111
Ishikawa	(0762) 40-3888
Iwate	(0196) 37-0110
Kagawa	(0878) 68-0111
Kagoshima	(099) 250-4040
Kanagawa	(045) 843-7110
Kitami	(0157) 61-0521
Kōchi	(0888) 85-0111
Kumamoto	(096) 380-3900
Kushiro	(0154) 51-2166
Kyoto	(075) 682-0111
Mie	(0592) 34-0110
Miyagi	(022) 288-0110
Miyazaki	(0985) 52-3900
Muroran	(0143) 87-0110
Nagano	(026) 223-1100
Nagasaki	(0958) 57-3900
Nara	(0742) 62-0111
Niigata	(025) 281-0111
Obihiro	(0155) 33-8171
Ōita	(0975) 68-2377
Okayama	(086) 272-4949
Okinawa	(098) 877-9163
Osaka	(06) 6577-0111
Saga	(0952) 62-3900
Saitama	(048) 651-0111
Sapporo	(011) 857-8138
Shiga	(0775) 44-0111
Shimane	(0852) 37-1224
Shizuoka	(054) 264-1110
Tochigi	(028) 659-3311
Tokushima	(0886) 55-0111
Tokyo	(03) 5395-0111

Tokyo (Tama)	(0423) 39-0111
Tottori	(0857) 27-4949
Toyama	(0764) 25-7373
Wakayama	(0734) 74-0111
Yamagata	(0236) 24-0110
Yamaguchi	(0839) 72-4949
Yamanashi	(0552) 41-0111

Counseling and Support Groups by Prefecture and Region

Kantō Area

AIDS Hotline	(03) 3359-2477
AMDA: International Medical Information Center	(03) 5285-8088
AMI Counseling	(03) 3448-1272
Al-Anon	(03) 3829-4402
Alcoholics Anonymous	(03) 3971-1471
Childbirth and Parenting	(03) 3461-8425
Co-Dependents	(03) 3423-2067
International Friends (gay support)	(03) 5693-4569
Japan HIV Center	(03) 5259-0256
Japan Help Line	(0120) 461-1997
Japan Hotline	(03) 3586-0110
TCCS—TELL Community Counseling Services	(03) 3780-0336
TELL—Tokyo English Life Line	(03) 5721-4347, 4455
Tokyo Alcoholics Anonymous	(03) 3971-1471
Tokyo English Lifeline HIV/AIDS	(03) 5221-4334
Tokyo Metropolitan Government's Foreign Resident's Advisory Center	(03) 5320-7744

Kansai Area

AMDA: International Medical Information
  Center   (06) 6636-2333
International Counselling Center   (078) 856-2201

Kyushu

Rainbow Plaza   (093) 661-7344

Aomori

St. Ursula Convent Center   (0178) 22-1463

Aichi

Tomo no Kai   (052) 953-9480

Chiba

Hand-in-Hand Chiba   (043) 224-2154

Fukuoka

Living in Asia Association   (092) 716- 0577

Gunma

Friends: Migrant Workers' Support
  Committee   (0270) 26-6460
Partner   (0270) 235-0110

Hiroshima

World Ship   (0849) 24-4435

Hokkaido

Association to Protect Human
   Rights of Foreigners in Japan   (011) 251-7834

Hyogo

NGO Network to Foreigners'
   Assistance Kobe   (078) 232-1290

Kanagawa

Catholic Diocese of Yokohama Solidarity
   Center for Migrants   (044) 549-7678
Jujodori Clinic   (0462) 74-5884
Kanagawa City Union   (044) 555-3411
Kanagawa International Association   (045) 896-2626
Kobayashi International Clinic   (0462) 63-1380
Korean Desk, Solidarity Center
   for Migrants   (044) 555-3477
Minatomachi Clinic   (045) 453-3673
Philippine Desk, Catholic Diocese of
   Yokohama Solidarity Center for Migrants (044) 549-7670
Yokohama Bar Association Consultation
   Service for Foreigners   (045) 211-7700
Yokosuka Chūō Clinic   (0468) 23-8691

Kyoto

Asian People Together   (075) 451-6522

Kumamoto

Camstaka: Society for Living
   Together with Foreigners   (096) 352-3030

Miyagi

Miyagi Foreigners' Problems Study Group in Miyagi	(022) 225-5108

Osaka

Asian Friend	(06) 6634-2127
Center for Multicultural Information and Assistance	(06) 6941-5734
Committee for International Cooperation	(06) 6941-4999
Korean Rights Group Japan	(06) 6715-2651
Sakai Catholic Church	(0722) 52-1498

Saitama

119 Network for Foreigners	(048) 834-0287
International Exchange Center Open House	(048) 827-0055

Shizuoka

Casa de Amigos Tobu	(0559) 81-3599
Forum on Asia in Shizuoka	(054) 273-3884
The Society for Human Rights of Foreigners in the Shidahaibara District	(054) 628-3084

Tokyo

Catholic Tokyo International Center	(03) 3636-1981
Christian Coalition on Refugee and Migrant Issues	(03) 3207-7801
East Tokyo Occupational Safety and Health Center	(03) 3683-9765
FLU (Zenrokyo-NGLU Foreign Laborers Union)	(03) 3235-3955

Fureai Koto Union	(03) 3638-3366
Foreign Residents Advisory Center	(03) 5320-7744
Group Akakabu	(03) 3940-6359
Hirano Kameido Himawari Clinic	(03) 5609-1823
International Legal Labor Union BRIGHT	(03) 3590-9110
Keihin Union	(03) 3762-5781
Lawyers Association for Foreign Labors' Rights	(03) 3305-0555
National Union of General Workers—Tokyo South	(03) 3434-0669
Santama General Labor Union	(042) 526-0061
Shibuya Harajuku Society for Life and Rights	(03) 5273-5065
Tokyo Bar Association Tokyo Center for Human Rights for Foreigners	(03) 3581-2302
Tokyo Nikkei's Employment Service Center	(03) 3836-1090
Voluntary Group Counseling and Assistance for Students from Abroad	(03) 3465-7550
Zentōitsu Workers Union	(03) 3836-9061

Yamanashi

OASIS (Yamanashi Human Rights Network for Foreigners)	(0552) 52-1244

Medical Services

Tokyo

Asian Students Cultural Association	(03) 3946-2171
Association of Medical Doctors for Asia	(03) 5285-8088
American Pharmacy	(03) 3271-4034
Central Clinic	(03) 3571-2841

International Catholic Hospital (Seibo Byōin)	(03) 3951-1111
International Clinic	(03) 3583-7831
Japanese Red Cross Medical Center	(03) 3400-1311
Jikei University Hospital	(03) 3433-1111
Juntendō University Hospital	(03) 3813-3111
Keiō University Hospital	(03) 3353-1211 (day)
	(03) 3353-1208 (eve.)
Kyorin University Hospital	(0422) 47-5511
Medical Dispensary	(03) 3434-5817
Musashino Red Cross Hospital	(0422) 32-3111
National Cancer Center	(03) 3542-2511
National Medical Clinic	(03) 3473-2057
Roppongi Pharmacy	(03) 3403-8880
St. Luke's International Hospital	(03) 3541-5151
Saiseikai Central Hospital	(03) 3451-8211
Sannō Clinic	(03) 3402-3151
The Second National Tokyo Hospital	(03) 3411-0111
Tokyo British Clinic	(03) 5458-6099
Tokyo Childbirth Education Association	(03) 3440-1657
Tokyo Clinic Dental Office	(03) 3431-4225
Tokyo Maternity Clinic	(03) 3403-1861
Tokyo Medical and Surgical Clinic	(03) 3436-3028
Tokyo Metropolitan Hiroo General Hospital	(03) 3444-1181
Tokyo Metropolitan Police Hospital	(03) 3263-1371
Tokyo Sanitarium Hospital (Tokyo Eisei Byōin)	(03) 3392-6151
Tokyo University Hospital	(03) 3815-5411
Tokyo Women's Medical College Hospital	(03) 3353-8111

Yokohama

Bluff Clinic	(045) 641-6961 (day)
	(045) 641-6964 (eve.)

Seishindō Pharmacy	(045) 314-9009
Yokohama City University Hospital	(045) 261-5656

Kobe

Kobe Adventist Hospital	(078) 981-0161
Kobe Central Municipal Hospital	(078) 302-4321
Kobe Kaisei Hospital	(078) 871-5201
Konan Hospital	(078) 851-2161
Miyaji Hospital	(078) 451-1221
Rokkō Island Hospital	(078) 858-1111

Religious Organizations in Tokyo

Bahai Faith	(03) 3209-7521
Church of Christ	(03) 3291-0478
Church of Jesus Christ of Latter-Day Saints	(03) 3496-6337
Church of Saint Mary's	(03) 3396-0305
Denenchōfu Lutheran Church	(03) 3721-4716
First Church of Christ Scientist	(03) 3499-3951
Franciscan Chapel Center	(03) 3401-2141
Friends Jidō Center	(03) 3203-7245
Full Gospel Tokyo Church	(03) 3357-2106
International Christian University Church	(0422) 33-3323
Islamic Center Japan	(03) 3460-6169
Japan Buddhist Federation	(03) 3437-9275
Japan Islamic Congress Majid	(03) 3205-1313
Japan Lutheran Church	(03) 3261-5266
Japan Muslim Association	(03) 3370-3476
Jewish Community of Japan	(03) 3400-2559
Jinja Honchō (United Shinto Shrines)	(03) 3379-8011
Kanto Plains Baptist Church	(0425) 51-1915
New Otani Garden Chapel	(03) 3265-1111

Ochanomizu Christian Center	(03) 3296-1001
Orthodox Church	(03) 3295-6879
Russian Orthodox Church	(03) 3341-2281
St. Alban's Anglican Episcopal Church	(03) 3431-8534
St. Andrew's Church	(03) 3431-2822
St. Anselm's Priory	(03) 3491-5461
St. Ignatius Church	(03) 3263-4584
St. Luke's Chapel	(03) 3541-5151
St. Paul Evangelical Lutheran Church	(03) 3261-3740
Salvation Army	(03) 3237-0881
Shalom Church Shinjuku	(03) 3371-7558
Shibuya Catholic Church	(03) 3463-5881
Sri Sathya Shi Center	(03) 3447-0408
Tokyo Baptist Church	(03) 3461-8425
Tokyo Lutheran Church	(0422) 55-1682
Tokyo Mosque	(03) 3469-0284
Tokyo Union Church	(03) 3400-0047
Tsukiji Honganji	(03) 3843-9511
Watch Tower Bible and Tract Society	(03) 3453-0404
West Tokyo Union Church	(0422) 33-0993
Yokota Baptist Church	(0425) 53-2577
Yokota Church of Christ	(0425) 52-7964

Donations

The following organizations in Tokyo accept used items:

Emmaus	(03) 3920-9118
The Family Christian Fellowship Organization	(03) 3315-3902
Salvation Army	(03) 3237-0881
Sankyū-Kai	(03) 3874-1269

International Schools

American School in Japan
1-1-1 Nomizu, Chōfu-shi, Tokyo 182-0031
Tel (0422) 34-5300, Fax (0422) 34-5308
• *Grades K–12*

American School in Japan
2-15-5 Aobadai, Meguro-ku, Tokyo 150-0042
Tel (03) 3461-4523, Fax (03) 3461-2505
• *Nursery–Kindergarten*

Aoba-Japan International School
2-10-7 Miyamae, Suginami-ku, Tokyo 168-0081
Tel (03) 3335-6620, Fax (03) 3332-6930
• *Nursery–Grade 9*

Aoba-Japan International School, Meguro Campus
2-10-34 Aobadai, Meguro-ku, Tokyo 153-0042
Tel (03) 3461-1442, Fax (03) 3463-9873
• *Nursery–Kindergarten*

British School in Tokyo
1-21-18 Shibuya, Shibuya-ku, Tokyo 150-0002
Tel (03) 5467-4321, Fax (03) 5467-4322
• *Grades K–6*

Canadian Academy in Japan
4-1 Kōyō-chō Naka, Higashi-Nada-ku, Kobe-shi, Hyōgo 658-0032
Tel (078) 857-0100, Fax (078) 857-3250
• *Grades K–12*

Christian Academy in Japan
1-2-14 Shinkawa-chō, Higashi-Kurume-shi, Tokyo 203-0013
Tel (0424) 71-0022, Fax (0424) 76-2200
• *Grades K–12*

Fukuoka International School
3-18-50 Momochi, Sawara-ku, Fukuoka-shi, Fukuoka 814-0006
Tel (092) 841-7601, Fax (092) 841-7602
• *Grades K–12*

Hiroshima International School
3-49-1 Kurakake, Asakita-ku, Hiroshima-shi, Hiroshima 739-1743
Tel (082) 843-4111, Fax (082) 843-6399
• *Grades K–8*

Hokkaido International School
1-55, 5-jō, 19 chōme, Hiragishi, Toyohira-ku, Sapporo-shi, Hokkaido 062-0435
Tel (011) 816-5000, Fax (011) 816-2500
• *Preschool–Grade 12*

International School of the Sacred Heart
4-3-1 Hiroo, Shibuya-ku, Tokyo 150-0012
Tel (03) 3400-3951, Fax (03) 3400-3496
• *Grades K–12*

Kansai Christian School
951 Tawaraguchi-chō, Ikoma-shi, Nara 630-0243
Tel (0743) 74-1781, Fax (0743) 74-1781
• *Grades 1–12*

Kyoto International School
317 Kitawara-chō, Nakadachiuri-sagaru, Yoshiyamachi-dōri, Kamigyō-ku, Kyoto 602-8247
Tel (075) 451-1022, Fax (075) 451-1023
• *Grades K–9*

Marist Brothers International School
1-2-1 Chimori-chō, Suma-ku, Kobe-shi, Hyōgo 654-0072
Tel (078) 732-6266, Fax (078) 732-6268
• *Grades K–12*

Nagoya International School
2686 Minamihara, Nakashidami, Moriyama-ku, Aichi 463-0002
Tel (052) 736-2025, Fax (052) 736-3883
• *Nursery–Grade 12*

Nishimachi International School
2-14-7 Moto-Azabu, Minato-ku, Tokyo 106-0046
Tel (03) 3451-5520, Fax (03) 3456-0197
• *Grades K–9*

Okinawa Christian School
P. O. Box 6, Yomitan-son, Okinawa 904-0391
Tel (098)-958-3000, Fax (098)-958-6279
• *Grades K–12*

Osaka International School
4-4-16 Onohara-Nishi, Mino-shi, Osaka 562-0032
Tel (0727) 27-5050, Fax (0727) 27-5055
• *Grades K–12*

Saint Joseph International School
85 Yamate-chō, Naka-ku, Yokohama-shi, Kanagawa 231-0862
Tel (045) 641-0065, Fax (045) 641-6572
• *Nursery–Grade 12*

Saint Mary's International School
1-6-19 Seta, Setagaya-ku, Tokyo 158-8668
Tel (03) 3709-3411, Fax (03) 3707-1950
• *Boys Grades K–12*

Saint Maur International School
83 Yamate-chō, Naka-ku, Yokohama-shi, Kanagawa 231-8654
Tel (045) 641-5751, Fax (045) 641-6688
• *Grades K–12*

Saint Michael's International School

3-17-2, Nakayamate-dōri, Chūō-ku, Kobe-shi, Hyōgo 650-0004
Tel (078) 231-8885, Fax (078) 231-8899
• *Grades 1–6*

Santa Maria School

2-2-4 Minami Tanaka, Nerima-ku, Tokyo 177-0035
Tel (03) 3904-0517, Fax (03) 3904-0552
• *Grades K–6*

Seisen International School

1-12-15 Yōga, Setagaya-ku, Tokyo 158-0097
Tel (03) 3704-2661, Fax (03) 3701-1033
• *Girls Grades K–12*

Tohoku American School

4-8-1 Komatsushima, Aoba-ku, Sendai-shi, Miyagi 981-0903
Tel (022) 234-8567, Fax (022) 272-7161
• *Grades 1–9*

Tokyo International Learning Community

6-30-50 Ōsawa, Mitaka-shi, Tokyo 181-0015
Tel (0422) 31-9611, Fax (0422) 31-9648
• *School for special needs*

Tokyo Union Church Preschool

5-7-7 Jingūmae, Shibuya-ku, Tokyo 150-0001
Tel (03) 3400-1579, Fax (03) 3400-1942
• *Ages 3–6*

Yokohama International School

258 Yamate-chō, Naka-ku, Yokohama-shi, Kanagawa 231-0862
Tel (045) 622-0084, Fax (045) 621-0379
• *Grades K–12*

Japanese Colleges
with Special Programs for Foreigners

Asia University Institute for Japanese Studies
5-24-10 Sakai, Musashino-shi, Tokyo 180-8629
Tel (0422) 54-3111, Fax (0422) 36-4869

Dōshisha University
Imadegawa-dōri, Karasuma Higashi-iru, Kamigyō-ku, Kyoto 602-8580
Tel (075) 251-3260, Fax (075) 251-3057

International Christian University
3-10-2 Ōsawa, Mitaka-shi, Tokyo 181-8585
Tel (0422) 35-3038

International University of Japan
Division of Education Affairs
Yamato-machi, Minami-Uonuma-gun, Niigata 949-7277
Tel (0257) 79-1111, Fax (0257) 79-4441

Jōchi University (Sophia University)
Faculty of Comparative Culture
7-1 Kioi-chō, Chiyōda-ku, Tokyo 102-8554
Tel (03) 3238-4018, Fax (03) 3238-3262

Kansai University of Foreign Studies (Kansai Gaidai)
Asian Studies Program
16-1 Nakamiyahigashino-chō, Hirakata-shi, Osaka 573-1001
Tel (072) 805-2831, Fax (072) 805-2830

Keiō University
2-15-45 Mita, Minato-ku, Tokyo 108-8345
Tel (03) 3453-4511, Fax (03) 5427-1638

Kōnan University
8-9-1 Okamoto, Higashi-Nada-ku, Kobe-shi, Hyōgo 658-8501
Tel (078) 435-2322, Fax (078) 435-2557

Kwansei Gakuin University
International Program, 1-1-155 Uegahara, Nishinomiya-shi, Hyōgo 662-0891
Tel (0798) 554-6131, Fax (0798) 51-0954

Nagoya Gakuin University
Institute for Japanese Language and Culture
1350 Kamishinano-chō, Seto-shi, Aichi 480-1298
Tel (0561) 42-0737, Fax (0561) 41-1147

Nanzan University
Center for Japanese Studies
18 Yamazato-chō, Shōwa-ku, Nagoya-shi, Aichi 466-8673
Tel (052) 832-3111, Fax (052) 833-6985

Obirin University
3758 Tokiwa-machi, Machida-shi, Tokyo 194-0294
Tel (042) 797-2661, Fax (042) 797-0790

Reitaku University
2-1-1 Hikarigaoka, Kashiwa-shi, Chiba 277-8686
Tel (0471) 73-3601, Fax (0471) 73-1100

Ritsumeikan University
International Center
56-1 Tōji-in Kitamachi, Kita-ku, Kyoto 603-8577
Tel (075) 465-1111, Fax (075)-465-8160

Seinan Gakuin University
International Division
6-2-92 Nishijin, Sawara-ku, Fukuoka-shi, Fukuoka 814-8511
Tel (092) 823-3346, Fax (092) 823-3334

Waseda University

International Division
1-7-14-404 Nishi-Waseda, Shinjuku-ku, Tokyo 169-0051
Tel (03) 3207-1454, Fax (03) 3202-8638

Real Life in Japan

Following are several stories and suggestions from people like yourself who have spent time living in Japan. Thanks to everyone who sent material for inclusion! Feel free to send any cautionary tales and helpful tips you might have to the e-mail addresses listed on the copyright page of this book.

Burnables go out on Tuesdays and Fridays. Yes, styrofoam is "burnable" but plastic water bottles aren't. Clear bags only. Recyclables go twice monthly. Split your PET bottles, drink cans, food cans, and remaining plastics. Pretend you don't have anything that doesn't fit into these categories. If you do, put it in an outdoor cupboard. If your garbage is still sitting there at the end of the day with a big red sticker on it, wait until nightfall. Now run out and get it wearing a hat and coat (that aren't yours). Contemplate your wrongdoings and analyze the "garbage guide" more closely. Better luck next time.

* * * * *

Needing a cheap bicycle, I picked up one that had been lying for several weeks next to an informal garbage dump in a Tokyo backstreet. Some oil and a fresh coat of paint—good as new! I used it happily for almost a year, but one night as I started home on it from the station bike-lot, two policemen emerged from the shadows and arrested me! Seems the bike had been stolen. I pleaded ignorance and got off with a warning. Moral: If the abandoned bike you covet has a registration medallion, go to the police station and see if it has been reported stolen before you consider it yours.

* * * * *

Multiple-trip tickets (*kaisūken*) save about 10 percent of the price for anywhere that you go on the train frequently, or even not so frequently—11 times in three months. Besides saving money you also save time by not having to stop and buy tickets each entry. On some routes, there are rush-hour and non-rush-hour varieties. In Tokyo the JR "within-the-Yamanote" tickets are especially handy.

* * * * *

There are several kinds of sleeping trains (*shindaisha*) for long trips. My favorite is a bed-size piece of floor with low partitions, a light, a window, and a small blanket—cheaper than a private room and more comfortable than a reclining chair, two other options. It's also cheaper than the Shinkansen, and saves you a hotel room.

* * * * *

After turning a morning meeting into a laugh-off for my coworkers with what I thought was a perfectly reasonable expression, my senior there taught me a valuable lesson that is sometimes overlooked in books. As much of the language is based on the speaker and the situation around them, my friend advised me, "When you study your Japanese, be careful that you are not speaking like a teen-aged girl." Sage advice, for any language.

* * * * *

We exchanged large amounts of yen on days when the yen rate was high; that really saved us quite a bundle. . . . I applied for an international driver's license while I was in the States, which helped us get around the island. Driving on the left side is really kind of nice.

* * * * *

The slurping of noodles is one of the few unabashedly natural sounds heard and even celebrated in Japan. Auditory bodily functions are, like most everything else, kept hidden or discreetly out of earshot. There are sound machines in the toilet stalls of the women's bathroom at the large corporation where I work. One press of a button and rushing rivers replace other less decorous emissions. But not the slurp. The louder the slurp, the more satisfaction it implies. It is downright rude not to slurp your noodles.

* * * * *

A trip to the local bathhouse, or *sentō*, reveals much more than skin. At the sento you can experience an atmosphere where individuals bathe together (separated by sex, though they didn't use to be), exchanging local gossip and cementing community bonds. The bather approaches his or her task with singular concentration. Every limb must be scrubbed, every inch of the body covered in a thick lather that the bather has worked up by passing a washcloth back and forth across the body in endless repetitions. Then the bucket is filled up with hot water and dumped over the body to rinse it completely. The process is repeated three times—this before one is allowed to get into the tubs, which are purely for soaking. There's an expression for the closeness one feels when bathing. It's *hadaka no tsukiai*, or "skinship."

* * * * *

Two useful Japanese cloths to know about. First, the *furoshiki*, or square carrying cloth; it is one of the most remarkable Japanese appliances yet one of the simplest. It's a bit like that folded bandana that hobos would hang from the end of a shoulder pole. But in Japan the *furoshiki* is elegant as well as functional. Use it to carry gifts, lunches, books, a change of clothing. *Furoshiki* come in all different patterns, some of them quite alluring. Second, the *tenugui*, a long, thin "washtowel" that you use in the Japanese bath. First you soap it up and rub it across your body to clean yourself. Then you rinse it out (thoroughly) and hold it over your private parts as you make your way to the communal soaking tub. Then you ball it up and wear it on your head as you soak in the tub, using it as fashion accessory and sweatmop. Finally, when the bath is done, you use the *tenugui* to dry yourself off, constantly wringing it out and rubbing it across your body until all the moisture from the bath is absorbed. Then wrap your *tenugui* with your toiletries in a *furoshiki* and walk back to your sleeping quarters, clean and relaxed.

* * * * *

The summer heat in Japan is debilitating, but the humidity factor is even worse. Walking outside in midsummer, one is bound to fry and soak at the same time. The solution is simple: a parasol. Yesterday my husband handed me one as we walked out the door. It was made of white cotton and had a frilly lace border and a carved bamboo handle. Walking the streets of Tokyo under my parasol, I grew to like the feeling of being somewhat hidden beneath its veil. I was greeted warmly by other parasol-toting women who nodded approvingly at my UV-resistant net, as if we were all members of a secret society of modern-day suffragettes. So on hot, clear, sunny days in Japan, don't forget to take your umbrella . . . er, parasol.

* * * * *

Maintain a sense of humor. If you can find it on your radio dial, listening to broadcasts of "Doctor Demento" can really be a great escape from the hurly-burly of Japan life. Find a dedicated family member or friend from back home to send videotapes of your favorite TV programs. Then, pass the tapes around to your friends; you'll be a hero! If you have feet of size, bring your own slippers and shoes from home. But no matter what you do, your heels will hang painfully off the back of those awful plastic bath-room slippers.

* * * * *

Really try to learn the language, especially all of the *kana* syllabic characters and a couple hundred *kanji*. Even though station names and lots of signage are in English, it is so much more convenient (and satisfying) to be able to deduce meanings on your own. The best approach is to not be overwhelmed by the sheer number of characters. There are about four dozen syllabic characters (in each of two parallel but different systems), so study them in groups of about five per night. Test yourself constantly while you're out walking around or riding the trains. You'll be surprised to see how quickly you begin to recognize the same character over and over again. There are books you can use too, but the best approach is to write the characters over and over again.

Notes

Notes

Notes

OTHER TITLES OF INTEREST FROM STONE BRIDGE PRESS

*Going to Japan on Business: Protocol, Strategies, and Language
for the Corporate Traveler* (3rd edition)
by Christalyn Brannen

Doing Business with Japanese Men: A Woman's Handbook
by Christalyn Brannen and Tracey Wilen

The Rice-Paper Ceiling: Breaking through Japanese Corporate Culture
by Rochelle Kopp

Japanese Beyond Words: How to Walk and Talk Like a Native Speaker
by Andrew Horvat

Kanji Pict-o-Graphix: Over 1,000 Japanese Kanji and Kana Mnemonics
by Michael Rowley

A Homestay in Japan: "Nihon to no Deai"
by Caron Allen with Natsumi Watanabe

Tokyo Q 2001–2002: Annual Guide to the City
by Tokyo Q Staff with Rick Kennedy

Little Adventures in Tokyo: 39 Thrills for the Urban Explorer
by Rick Kennedy

The Inland Sea
by Donald Richie

The Donald Richie Reader: 50 Years of Writing on Japan
by Donald Richie, edited by Arturo Silva

The Broken Bridge: Fiction from Expatriates in Literary Japan
edited by Suzanne Kamata

One Hot Summer in Kyoto
by John Haylock

STONE BRIDGE PRESS, P. O. BOX 8208, BERKELEY, CA 94707

To comment on this book or to receive a free catalogue of other books
about Japan and Japanese culture, contact Stone Bridge Press at
sbp@stonebridge.com / 1-800-947-7271 / www.stonebridge.com